Discovering My Autism

of related interest

Asperger's Syndrome
A Guide for Parents and Professionals
Tony Attwood
ISBN 1 85302 577 1

Through the Eyes of Aliens
A Book about Autistic People
Jasmine Lee O'Neill
ISBN 1 85302 710 3

Autism: An Inside-Out Approach
An Innovative Look at the Mechanics of 'Autism'
and its Developmental 'Cousins'
Donna Williams
ISBN 1 85302 387 6

Autism and Sensing
The Unlost Instinct
Donna Williams
ISBN 1 85302 612 3

Children with Autism, Second Edition
Diagnosis and Interventions to Meet Their Needs
Colwyn Trevarthen, Kenneth Aitken, Despina Papoudi and Jacqueline Robarts
ISBN 1 853 02 555 0

The ADHD Handbook
A Guide for Parents and Professionals
Alison Munden and Jon Arcelus
ISBN 1 85302 756 1

From Thoughts to Obsessions
Obsessive Compulsive Disorder in Children and Adolescents
Per Hove Thomsen
ISBN 1 85302 721 9

Discovering My Autism
Apologia Pro Vita Sua
(with Apologies to Cardinal Newman)

Edgar Schneider

Jessica Kingsley Publishers
London and Philadelphia

First published in the United Kingdom in 1999 by
Jessica Kingsley Publishers Ltd,
116 Pentonville Road,
London N1 9JB, England
and
325 Chestnut Street,
Philadelphia, PA 19106, USA.

www.jkp.com

Copyright © 1999 Edgar R.G. Schneider

Library of Congress Cataloging in Publication Data
Schneider, Edgar, 1932–
Discovering my autism : apologia pro vita sua (with apologies to Cardinal Newman) /
Edgar Schneider.
p.   cm.
ISBN 1-85302-724-3 (pbk. : alk. paper)
1. Schneider, Edgar, 1932–   . 2. Autism--Patients--Biography.
I. Title.
RC553.A88S36 1999
616.89'82'0092--dc21
[B]
98-42738
CIP

British Library Cataloguing in Publication Data
Schneider, Edgar
Discovering my autism : apologia pro vita sua (with apologies to Cardinal Newman)
1. Schneider, Edgar 2. Autism – Patients – Biography
3. Attention-deficit-disordered adults – Biography
I. Titles
616.8'982'0092

ISBN 1 85302 724 3

Printed and Bound in Great Britain by
Athenaeum Press, Gateshead, Tyne and Wear

Contents

To Father Neil Doherty, who was instrumental in getting me to write this story; to Jan Cook, my very good friend who was instrumental in my getting involved with autism advocacy; and to Rosalyn Lord, who was instrumental in getting my story published

Prologue

The poet Alexander Pope, in *An Essay on Man*, offered this admonition: 'Know then thyself, presume not God to scan.' Indeed, Thales, considered to be the founder of Greek philosophy and mathematics, believed that knowing oneself was the most difficult thing to learn. The first half of what Pope wrote is undeniably excellent advice. The question is: how to do it?

Introspection is generally not reliable, because any image that we have of ourselves has got to be, by its very nature, self-serving. We look in the mirror and see a certain picture. The one on the driver's licence may very well be closer to the mark. The views of our friends and acquaintances may not be reliable either because they are colored by an opinion of us acquired over time.

On the other hand, for those of us who are fortunate to have this happen, something will come into our lives from a source that has no axe to grind one way or another, and to which we can relate what we do know to be factual. Such an experience happened to me recently, and gave me insights into why I do what I do, why I think and believe as I do, and why I interact with others as I do, not only now but also for all of my past life. It explained so many things about me that had previously been enigmas, even to myself.

I discussed all of this with the pastor of my church. He suggested to me, after hearing this story, that I write it. I have done just that, not only for those who might like to know me better, but also as catharsis for myself.

I should like to start with a past incident that could be said to have marked the onset of this process of self-revelation. It took place at that time at which the classical epic poems began their stories: the 'middle of things'.

The Determining Time Period

In June 1978, while living in upstate New York, I suffered a nervous breakdown. It was the result of intense pressure by my immediate management at work. Before this, I had always been considered an exemplary employee. My skills as a mathematician and scientific computer programmer were prized and rewarded. However, in the few years prior to this, my memory and concentration started to fail, causing me to make stupid mistakes and suffer declining productivity. My speech, which had been concise, began to become rambling, often digressing from the point I was trying to make. I also found it impossible to stick to a task for any appreciable length of time.

It may very well have been the onset of an attention deficit disorder (ADD). They are just now discovering that this condition can arise in adults, and not, as they had thought previously, only in children. Of course, at that time, nobody had any inkling that this might be the case.

The company I worked for has an excellent program for dealing with employees whose performance suddenly takes a downward turn, especially if it is due to the onset of some disability. If they had applied it in my case, I would never have had that breakdown. One facet of that program is that, before the employee is put on notice, an effort must be made to determine if a medical contraindication exists.

Contrary to company policy, this was not done, so it would have made no difference if there had been any knowledge of adult onset of ADD. As a result, the pressure on me was increased. My family situation added to the pressure. I had three children, all still in school, and my wife needed an operation. On that last item, if I had to change jobs due to being fired, or having even resigned, then any medical benefits in a new job would almost invariably have excluded my wife's pre-existing condition.

At this point, a disclaimer and a bit of explanation might be in order. In no way should the previous paragraph be taken to imply that anything my family did or did not do was the cause of my breakdown.

Before this incident, I had encountered a number of reversals in my fortunes of no small magnitude. In each case, I fought back as much as my resources allowed. If the fight proved successful, all well and good. If not, I retrenched and plotted another course for my life. If this retrenchment caused any hardship, I bore it with equanimity until such time as the new course came to fruition.

In any case, like a cat, I invariably landed on my feet. When I was an officer in the Army, one of my sergeants said of me, 'He's the only man I ever met who could fall into a slit-trench latrine and come out smelling like roses'. In other words, I was always a survivor. I always credited this to the fact that, on my mother's side, my ancestry is Russian, and unquestionably, historically, they are a nation of survivors.

What was different in this case? Here, any hardships would also be borne by others, namely a wife and three children who depended on me. It was this that I found impossible to deal with, and that caused me to snap. The significance of this will be made clear later on.

About a month into my problems at work, I was finally able come to terms with the fact that perhaps I needed some kind of professional help. I tried to make an appointment to see a private psychiatrist, if only hoping that a doctor of mine could present evidence to the company of the requisite medical contraindication. However, all of their waiting lists precluded seeing one prior to the deadline for shaping up or shipping out (as they say in the Army).

All of this proved too much and, in the month mentioned, I was taken by my wife to a crisis center at a local hospital that had a psychiatric facility. Once admitted, a psychiatrist was assigned to me.

I spent about two months in the hospital, during which time a number of psychotropic drugs were tried on me. My doctor chose one, Navane[1] for me to take after my discharge. Following a period of home convalescence, I returned to work on a part-time basis. Gradually, my work hours were increased and my Navane dosage was decreased. By the end of the year, I was working full-time and the Navane was discontinued. Since my doctor felt that the cause of my breakdown was situational, he told me that he did not need to see me any more.

The new management that I had was as understanding as my old one had been brutal, and it looked as though my glory years were returning. However, in a few months, the problems involving short-term memory and concentration (including attention to detail) started to appear again.

---

1   An anti-psychotic drug. At that time, anti-psychotic drugs were supposed to make a 'volatile' personality more 'stable', so they were called 'major tranquilizers'.

(Again, the classic symptoms of ADD.) I did not notice it, but others did, especially my new manager.

He talked with me about it at some length. I guess I had been in some denial because, when I was in the hospital, I noticed that everybody else that I met had been there at least once before, and I did not want to be a 'repeater'. My manager helped me talk it out, and, having decided to face reality, I decided, in the summer of 1979, to contact my psychiatrist once more.

He said that he believed me to be having another breakdown, but also was impressed by the fact that there were no external causes. My job was secure, and even my family situation was OK. My wife's surgery had corrected her problem, my daughter was in college on a scholarship, my oldest son had enlisted in the Marines, and my youngest son was doing well in middle school.

I can only guess that, just as internists call anything they cannot pinpoint a virus (if there is a fever) or an allergy (if there isn't one), psychiatrists would call someone schizophrenic when they do not know what else to call him. Anyhow, that is the diagnosis that was hung around my neck like the Ancient Mariner's albatross. Again, I was hospitalized for about two months, trying out various anti-psychotic drugs, until my doctor settled on Loxitane[2] (with Artane, which was used to ward off some of Loxitane's side-effects).

Perhaps I am being a bit harsh by implying that this incorrect diagnosis was the result of incompetence on the part of that initial psychiatrist. The state of knowledge of mental conditions was rather embryonic at that time, and some of the fine distinctions, that today enable practitioners to make the categorizations that are necessary for accurate diagnoses, were simply unknown at that time.

It did not help matters any that I have always possessed a number of unconventional personality characteristics. Not that they would render me socially outré, but arguably eccentric (in the literal sense of that word: off-center). Yet, although schizophrenics are eccentric, a person can be eccentric without being schizophrenic. This is a subtlety seemingly lost on many people, professionals in the field not excepted.

However, there were other factors involved. First, my adult-onset ADD (about which they could not have known at that time) caused me to be what they call tangential; in other words, when I talk about something, I go

2   Another anti-psychotic drug.

off on another topic before finishing the first. This is something schizophrenics do. For another thing, my thought processes had become somewhat illogical (a classic schizophrenia symptom), but this was a consequence of the medications that I was taking.[3] Lastly, I would, at times, hear my name being called and upon, turning around, nobody had done so. This was interpreted as 'auditory hallucinating'.

Eccentric, tangential, illogical, and hallucinatory: this added up to schizophrenia. In each case, the diagnosis could have gone there or another way. Considering that, in each case, the syndrome was used to point to schizophrenia shows why, to this day, with luck like that, I will not so much as risk a dollar for a lottery or raffle ticket. I will donate the price of the ticket, but will *not* buy it. I am convinced that, not only will I not win, but that some dreadful consequence will ensue.[4]

---

[3] There has to be a certain irony in the fact that the side-effects of certain medications mimic the symptoms of the illnesses they are supposed to be treating.

[4] This could also be considered a consequence of a corollary of Murphy's Law. The law: if anything can go wrong it will. The corollary: if your chances of being right are 50–50, then 9 times out of 10 you'll be wrong.

Aftermath

For a couple of years, I continued to try to work. However, my problems caused me to have to do things like look things up repeatedly, make sloppy mistakes in details, and have to take long periods of respite (the Loxitane made me periodically quite sleepy). Another effect of the Loxitane was loss of creative thinking (which had hitherto been a *forte* of mine) making it extremely difficult to get started on a task. All of this added up to low productivity, at a time when all companies were stressing this feature as a critical indicator of an employee's performance. After a series of consultations with my manager, my doctor, and the company doctor, I was persuaded to be placed on the corporation's medical disability retirement program.

My doctor tried me on a number of different medications, since the Loxitane was not improving me at all. Among these were Lithium[1] (which made me suicidal while I was taking it; I have never been suicidal otherwise) and MAO Inhibitors.

This latter item required a diet that was the closest thing to bread and water that I have ever been on.[2] To the amusement of the dietitians, I noticed, and made note of the fact, that the menus, reflecting my diet, that they gave me to fill out were color coded with a blue stripe which, in French, is *cordon bleu*.

My doctor also tried electric shock therapy. Like the other therapies, it did no good at all.

Since any mood disorder[3] was not really noticeable, even to those who knew me well, and, to any extent I might have had one, it was not particularly burdensome to me (I could always barricade myself by myself at home when it might have taken over), he took me off psychotropic

---

1 Normally used for treatment of bipolar disorder, which I have never had.
2 MAO stands for monoamine oxidase. These drugs can be deadly if a draconian diet is not strictly observed.
3 I never did find out what anyone meant by this. Any explanations that I have been given were short on specifics and were given in a manner mathematicians call 'hand-waving'.

drugs, but gave me a prescription for Xanax,[4] to be taken as needed for any occasional bouts with free-floating anxiety.

Unknown to me, Xanax contained an antidepressant. I knew that depression was *not* my problem because, whenever I would take an antidepressant, I would develop a real short fuse. The reason for this became clear to me quite recently.

When I read an article on the manic-depressive (bipolar) syndrome, I looked at the symptoms that described the manic phase and thought, 'My God! I'm probably manic all the time!' These symptoms included needing hardly any sleep, and having 'heightened thinking' (my mind is in constant overdrive, in the literal sense of that word, going at great speed with minimal effort on the engine's part). When one's mental state is so high, is there any wonder that an antidepressant, which raises it further, pushes it through the roof?

On a couple of occasions, in December 1982 and July 1983, I took the Xanax for occurrences of mild anxiety[5] and, each time, had a reaction that was, mistakenly it turns out, called a 'psychotic episode'. (See the previous paragraph.) They were so severe that, on each occasion, my wife had to call the police. After the second one, I was taken by the police to a local crisis center; my doctor was contacted and he had me admitted to the same hospital I had been in thrice before. The diagnosis of schizophrenia was confirmed, and I was put on Navane (with, what I called, a Cogentin[6] chaser). There have never been any more such episodes.

The Navane did stabilize my moods, but it was like living under water. My intellectual and aesthetic sensibilities were completely blunted and numbed,[7] and I found it almost impossible to talk to anyone, even about the weather.

My doctor and I later parted company over a disagreement as to his future plans for me. I felt that what he wanted me to do would jeopardize certain benefits, and he refused to explain those plans to me.

(I did not connect those seemingly psychotic episodes with the Xanax until years later, when another psychiatrist told me about the anti-

---

4   An anti-anxiety drug. These were formerly called 'minor tranquilizers'.

5   I would not have done so, had I known of the side-effects due to the antidepressant ingredient. In fact, I likely would never have taken it at all.

6   A medication to counteract certain side-effects of the Navane. This is similar to the Loxitane/Artane combination.

7   I have read of many creative artists and thinkers who could no longer create after taking antipsychotic drugs.

-depressant ingredient. At that time, I would have liked to have sued for malpractice, but have since learned that, because Xanax was so new at that time, this side-effect was not generally known to mental health practitioners.)

Resolution, of a Sort

After that, I went from one psychiatrist to another at the county mental health clinic. Each would see me approximately every three months for about fifteen minutes, ask how I had been doing, and write new prescriptions for my medications.

When I moved to South Florida in July 1992, I got a new psychiatrist who told me that if all I wanted was someone to keep me on Navane and Cogentin, then I should see someone else. He would not do it because he knew that those anti-psychotic drugs turned people into zombies and, for the length of time I had been taking them, I was ripe for tardive dyskinesia.[1]

In December 1992, he moved me over to Depakote, which acts as a mood stabilizer, and Buspar, an anti-anxiety drug.[2] The difference was dramatic. Those lost intellectual and aesthetic faculties returned, and then some. I have since done a great deal of writing (I was invited to lecture on one paper that I wrote), I have gone back into artsy photography, and I have sung with three concert choruses, the best of which is the Florida Philharmonic Chorus. I look upon my membership in that organization as the musical equivalent of my election to Phi Beta Kappa.

If I were still on Navane, not only would I not be doing these things, but there is also absolutely no possibility that I could have written this autobiography.

1   A disorder characterized by restlessness and involuntary rolling of the tongue or twitching of the face, trunk, or limbs. Usually occurs as a complication of long-term therapy with anti-psychotic drugs. Can be irreversible.
2   When I discontinued these, I actually felt much more relaxed.

Suspicions

One interesting thing is that, during all those years, only one professional person questioned my schizophrenia diagnosis. (A number of confirmed schizophrenics that I knew also did so, but I dismissed them as incompetent to make that judgement.) This was *not* any of those psychiatrists, but an MSW (Master of Social Work) therapist to whom I was assigned when I first started being treated at the county clinic. He told me that he doubted that diagnosis because I did not exhibit three symptoms that he considered bedrock to schizophrenia.

The first was being divorced from reality. He told me that, after only a few sessions, he saw that I obviously had a firm grasp of reality.

The second was that I did not hear voices. I told him that sometimes I would hear someone call my name when, upon turning around, nobody had done so (these were those so-called 'auditory hallucinations'). He said that was common to a lot of people, unlike, he told me, real schizophrenic auditory hallucinations, which would be voices telling me to do things, usually terrible things.

The third thing he told me is that I was not delusional. I told him that I fantasized a lot. Examples are: I was a great Wagnerian opera singer, or I was a genius mathematician who had discovered a counterexample to Fermat's Last Theorem (a much greater coup than finding the missing proof).[1] He told me that, while I might have fantasized about being such things, I did not *believe* that I was.

There were three factors that this therapist did not mention, but that I must. (These are also factors that made my last doctor question my initial diagnosis.)

The first is that the thought processes of schizophrenics are chaotic. One upshot of this is that they are always either forgetting to take their medicines or rationalizing for not doing so. (Psychiatrists are always

---

1 This is a rhetorical remark, used to make my point about fantasizing. I am quite aware that a proof has been found. Yet, there is one puzzlement about that proof. It requires mathematics that was unknown in Fermat's time. So, how did he prove it?

constantly telling caregivers to steadfastly oversee this.) Another is that they are ruled by their emotions.

My thought processes, on the other hand, through good times and bad, have been mathematically logical. I have also been told, by more than one person and on more than one occasion, that I put too high a premium on logic and rationality, giving short shrift to the emotions.

A third is that schizophrenics are grim individuals, without a sense of humor. They tend to look at the world around them in the most literal of terms. Once I had gotten off the Navane, my doctor told me that he noticed in me a highly-developed sense of humor, the type of which, I told him, stemmed from my observations of the incongruities and ambiguities in things (an insight I got from my high school geometry teacher).

One example of this came up from something that happened in my allergist's office. She kept jars of candy, for her patients, on her receptionist's counter. On one visit, I noticed there a can labeled 'inhalators'. Opening it, I saw some little yellow and green things that had strong lemon and lime odors. I proceeded to put one into my nostril when the nurse yelled, 'What are you doing that for? Those are gummy bears!' I showed her what the can said and she told me that it was just a container for those candies. I said, 'It's a damned good thing you didn't put them in a can labeled "suppositories".'

He noticed also that I love plays on words. In April of 1995, the Florida Grand Opera put on a production of Wagner's *Der Fliegende Holländer*.[2] I was part of an offstage male chorus they needed in the third act for the Dutchman's ship's crew. We did our performances in opera houses first in Miami and then in Ft Lauderdale. In each case, we sang in a closed room, where an assistant conductor followed the main conductor via a closed-circuit TV monitor, and our voices came out on stage via speakers.

At the first performance in Ft Lauderdale, many of us could not find our room (we all did so in time to sing), so, at the start of Act III, only half of us were there. The assistant conductor looked rather concerned. I said to him, 'Don't worry. Shouldn't a ghost ship have a skeleton crew?'

Like Queen Victoria, he was not amused, but my doctor, like everyone else to whom I have told that story, thought it was hilarious. (I mentioned above that I had an adolescent fantasy about singing Wagner in an opera house. Here, it finally came to pass.)

2   *The Flying Dutchman*

I must also note, in retrospect, that I have always been able to do two things that schizophrenics are not able to do. One is to easily make the transition from the particular to the general and *vice versa*. The other is to see the logical connection between two statements or arguments that are different but analogous. These capabilities proved to be essential to my facility with mathematics.

I asked that MSW therapist what he thought my actual problem was; he replied that he didn't know. After about a year, he told me that he had come around to believe that I probably was schizophrenic. This is because, I am sure, he, like everyone else, did not know what else to call it. He said he believed that, for schizophrenics, psychotherapy was not indicated, so he ended our sessions.

A Revelation

I did not myself question this diagnosis until the early spring of 1995. (I felt that my current doctor was not particularly comfortable either, for the same reasons. He called me *atypical*.)

At that time, I read an article[1] by Oliver Sacks called 'Prodigies' that aroused in me the great possibility that, for sixteen years, all of the professionals who had been treating me were dead wrong! I saw so much of myself in that article, it was uncanny. I immediately brought it to the attention of my doctor, and we spent three months discussing it before agreeing that I had been grossly misdiagnosed.

The subject of the article was: autistic *savants*. My doctor and I have agreed that, with near certainty, this is the correct diagnosis.

The title, as can be seen, gives scant indication as to the subject matter (not unusual for that periodical), and I would have passed it by had it not been for the subtitle, which reached out from the page and grabbed my attention. It asks the question: 'Can an artist make art without feeling it?' Put more generally, it might be asked, 'Since expressing emotion is what art is all about, can one express emotion through words and pictures, even emotion of great depth, without feeling it?' The answer, judging from my own life is: 'You had better believe it!'

The article itself does talk about being able to feel great emotion, but only through art (and, by extension, music, literature and other creative intellectual and aesthetic pursuits).

This is because, through the arts, emotions are translated into sights, sounds, and words. These can be understood and expressed via one's intellectual and aesthetic faculties and do not absolutely require any emotional capability of one's own.

1 Sacks, Oliver (January 9, 1995) 'Prodigies', *The New Yorker*, 44–65.

Recap of a Terrible Period

Before I continue, it might be to the point to sum up what I had to endure for all of those years because of the 'schizophrenia' label (which my doctor said 'we can forget about'). I had been tried out on just about every antipsychotic drug. (My doctor told me that mood stabilizers are *not* antipsychotics – not by a long shot!) I was tried out on Lithium and MAO inhibitors. I was tried out on shock treatments. Nobody who knows the truth now should be surprised that none of these worked on me, but I had to deal with almost every one of the unfortunate side-effects associated with those therapies.

Worst of all, I was considered by most as being unstable, unpredictable, possibly dangerous; if you will: 'crazy', someone who had to be put under some kind of control, chemically if not physically. My three children could not help but worry if they had inherited something awful which would come out in their early forties, as it had done with me. Of course, what had come out was ADD (attention deficit disorder), which can possibly be treated in a fairly simple manner.

When I had that schizophrenia label, there were two things that weighed heavily on my mind. Obviously, the first was that I had a severe mental disorder that had savaged, among other things, what I considered to be one of my most treasured mental faculties: my rationality. To make this worse, I actually still did have my rationality, so that I had full awareness of what I thought was happening.

The other concern came about when one of my psychiatrists told me that there is a strong hereditary component to schizophrenia. I had three kids, none of whom exhibited any symptoms. I had to wonder: since I came by my condition late in life, was there a time bomb ticking away inside each or any of them? My current doctor has told me that whatever evidence exists that autism might be inherited indicates that it is a recessive trait so that my kids would, at most, be carriers.

But even this might be a cause for needless worry. One area of agreement seems to be that autism is developed during the formative stages of the nervous system. This means that any ailments, which can cause neurological damage and that take place during those earlier years, could be the culprit, without having to have any genetic predisposition.

Consider what happened to me. At the age of two and one half, I was bitten by a rabid dog (no question about it; the dog was isolated and died of it) and I had to take the Pasteur series of injections. During the time when I was three or four years of age, I came down with, and managed to survive, both pertussis and scarlet fever. I have been told that the combination of any or all of these could quite easily have impeded proper neurological development or damaged what had already developed, so as to cause my autism. For me this was actually good news because it would tend to show that the probability of any of my descendants being autistic would be miniscule.

There is evidence of this in something that, from time to time, my late mother would tell me. She said that, up until that period of my young life, I had been a happy-go-lucky, outgoing, gregarious, and demonstrative child. From the age of four onward, I became withdrawn, uncommun-icative, and solitary. There is no doubt, at this time, in my own mind, that this coincided with the onset of my autism.

For this reason, I have come to strongly doubt that autism is inherited, in the sense of there existing an 'autism' gene. Perhaps there could be said to be an indirect genetic component, in the form of an inherited susceptibility to the neurological assaults that cause autism.

This kind of neurological history may also be the cause of my being constantly manic. (I have alluded to this earlier.) This causes me little concern because, while it may require other people to have to take me in small doses, I do get a great deal of joy out of living, in bad times as well as good.

Correlating my Past Life

I should like, at this point, to start to relate specific items in the article I read to myself. I must stress that, as my priest friend and my doctor did this with me, I did not just examine my current state or even my recent past, but searched my not inconsiderable long-term memory for incidents that reached back to my early childhood.

First, as far as being able to connect with other live human beings, male or female, I am an emotional idiot. (That last phrase is mine; the phrase commonly used in psychology is 'emotional deficit'.) It seems that, just as some people have an important physical component missing (eyes, limbs, etc.), I have an important component of the human psyche missing: the ability to connect emotionally with other human beings.

This, however, may be somewhat simplistic. We are not automata, totally devoid of *all* feeling. What we lack are the emotions that enable people to 'connect' with the emotions of other people. I do find myself as having experienced what I call the 'survival' emotions: fear and anger. The fact that autism takes away the social, connective emotions,[1] but leaves the survival emotions, sometimes rendering one asocial, could be considered as one of Mother Nature's sick jokes.

Yet, even these survival emotions are essentially solitary in nature and come only in response to what I feel are unwanted intrusions into my private cosmos (what people today call their 'space'). (This is analogous to a cat scratching and biting only when it either is cornered or feels itself mishandled.) I do often welcome the company and assistance of others, but, unless I do the welcoming (much more often than this might imply), I do tend to withdraw into myself.

One way in which this manifests itself is a way of doing things that could be called obsessive-compulsive, although not in the strict technical sense (I do not do things repetitiously). The best work that I have ever done I did as a 'one-man band', as I like to call it. Even when I sing in a chorus, I think of it as a conglomeration of soloists. The way I like to

1   Sometimes referred to as the 'intuitive' emotions.

function can best be described by a sign that my favorite automobile mechanic had in his service bay:

> Labor charges: $20 an hour
> If you watch: $30 an hour
> If you help: $50 an hour

I was asked by a teacher, whose specialty is autistic children, what my greatest fear was. After giving it a bit of thought, I had to say that it was fear of uncertainty. I have to have a plan for where I am going. When circumstances change, I can change my plan, but I need a plan to change from.

Technically, I am not a *savant*, as was the subject of Dr Sack's article. These are people who have the communication and other difficulties usually associated with autism, but possess some superhuman mental faculty. (They were referred to as 'idiot *savants*' prior to the first diagnosis of autism, c. 1950.) This is almost invariably of a 'mechanical' nature, such as multiplying large numbers or telling the day on which a particular date fell. I am part of a group called HFA.[2] Those of us with normal communication capabilities are said to have AS.[3] What we all share, of course, is the emotional deficit.

The person who could easily be called the poster girl for HFA is Temple Grandin, a professor of animal science at Colorado State University, with whom I have had limited correspondence. It was she who, after reading an earlier, shorter version of this autobiography, wrote to me that I was likely a person with AS. I took it as no small compliment, coming from her, that, 'Many Asperger people are intellectually gifted'.

I have a way, unless I know what I hear to be a bald-faced lie, of taking people at their word. I refer back to being able to express feelings through art and literature (opera libretti included), but not in direct communication with other people's feelings. (I still cannot fathom how the NT[4] manage to do that.) It is not that I am totally unfeeling, but that I just cannot 'read other people's signals'. I have no built-in signal decoder.

This can have good and bad ramifications. A popular lapel button and bumper sticker among young women today is, 'What part of "No" don't you understand?' I always understood. In fact, when a woman told me 'No'

---

2   An abbreviation for 'high-functioning autistic'.
3   An abbreviation for 'Asperger's Syndrome'.
4   An abbreviation for 'neurologically-typical', a jargon term for non-autistic people.

once, I did not ask her a second time. However, when a person says, 'I'll be all right', I've been led to understand that this may by code for, 'I need help'. My inability to tell the difference is, I suppose, what sometimes causes me to be thought of as being without compassion.

If people think of me as being non-communicative about my feelings, it is because I have never had any feelings to discuss. I can, however, communicate my ideas, but this has led to being criticized for 'intellectualizing' problems.

Sometimes I may appear to be overly suspicious of others. This is *not* your garden-variety paranoia. I wrote earlier of my fear of uncertainty and of my inability to discern accurately, in an intuitive manner, the true intentions of others. Being cognizant of the possible consequences of any miscalculation of those intentions is what gives rise to my wariness. Those who, in my experience, have been completely up front with me, I trust completely.

Psychologists tend to call excessive suspiciousness a defense mechanism; for me it has had to be a survival skill.

Does being unable to 'feel' preclude my discussing his or her feelings with an NT person? Absolutely not. If the other person can accurately describe those feelings in words, they become thoughts or ideas, and those I can deal with very well. In fact, as a bonus, I might very well enable the other person to sort out his or her problems and find a solution, because there will be no emotional baggage of mine injected into the discussion.

The autistic person might appear to others to be distant and unsympathetic. (I have, no doubt, appeared that way to many.) This, however, is not the case. He must be allowed to consider the problems and feelings of others with the tools that he has at his disposal, often in abundance.

It appears to me that kindness and generosity are extremely logical and rational. It is gratuitous cruelty that has no logic about it, and would seem to spring from the emotions untempered by any rationality whatsoever.

In connection with the article's subtitle, my wife has often heard me relate classic love stories to others (Orpheus and Euridice, Dido and Æneas, Francesca da Rimini and Paolo, Tristan and Isolde, etc., the last being my favorite). Those who have heard me were invariably moved by the way I told these tales. (I have been told that I am a very good storyteller.) My wife would ask me why I could not express such emotions in connection with real people. (This question was asked with increasing bitterness as the years went on.) Then, I didn't know why; I just couldn't. As a result, at those times, I did not know what to tell her.

For all of our life together, my wife complained about an 'emotional wall' that she said that I had around me. Considering what I know now, a more fitting metaphor would be a 'dry hole'. A wall can be either knocked down by the one outside, or pulled down by the one inside. Nothing thirst-quenching can ever be sucked out of a dry hole.

In connection with this, advice-to-the-lovelorn columns regularly feature letters complaining about frigid wives or 'cold fish' husbands. The answers always suggest counseling and imply that the offending spouses could change their ways by some act of the will or change in attitude. (Psychotherapy is often recommended.) I wonder how many marriage counselors would ever think of having that spouse evaluated for my type of autism.

An Interesting Aside

When I wrote about being able to express emotion through art when one does not feel such emotion, I thought about three of my favorite composers, whose music gave no clue whatsoever as to what their personalities were like (although there is no evidence that there was any autism involved). In fact, very much to the contrary; their music was quite the opposite of the kind of men they were.

One was Richard Wagner. His music dramas bristle with lofty, idealistic principles and tender, caring emotions. Yet in my view he was a totally unprincipled wretch who shamelessly used others, even those who virtually worshipped him and his music. One egregious example was the prominent conductor Hans von Bülow, who was responsible for getting Wagner's music heard at a time when powerful critics were against him. Wagner repaid him by stealing his wife and fathering three children by her before making an honest man of himself by marrying her. The worst of it is that he so mesmerized those admirers that they thought themselves among the favored for having been used by him.

Another is Anton Bruckner. His music is so huge and so powerful as to appear to want to envelope the entire universe. One would think that he had to be a man with an enormous ego with appetites to match. Very much to the contrary, he was a totally shy, humble, and self-effacing man who, as all his biographers seem to agree, really was celibate to the end of his days.

There is an amusing example of this. He once attended a concert at which one of his symphonies was to be performed. This is every conductor's nightmare, because temperamental composers have been known to boisterously interrupt concerts to complain loudly of the conductor's interpretation. Wanting to forestall this, the conductor of the evening, before the start of the concert, approached Bruckner and asked him how he would like his symphony conducted. Bruckner replied, 'Conduct it any way you like'.

The third is Richard Strauss. He wrote thundering tone poems (*Ein Heldenleben* and *Tod und Verklärung*[1] for example) and emotion-laden operas, such as *Salome* and *Elektra* (lust and hatred), or *Rosenkavalier* and *Ariadne auf Naxos*[2] (lost and newfound love). Yet, he had the personality one normally associates with accountants.[3] He married an operatic soprano with a volatile personality. Predictably, by all accounts, the marriage was rocky.

He wrote an autobiographical opera, *Intermezzo* (he cast himself in the baritone rôle). His wife, beside herself trying to get any display of emotion out of him, taunts him by telling him of an affair with some lover (the tenor, of course), to no avail. When, at the very end, he does get angry with her, she is overcome with joy.

I also must mention two men in the sciences whose brilliance in their respective fields is virtually unquestioned, yet who failed in every attempt that they made to try to form a close personal relationship. They are Albert Einstein and Bertrand Russell.

.

1   *A Hero's Life* and *Death and Transfiguration*.
2   *The Knight of the Rose* and *Ariadne on Naxos*
3   With apologies to accountants who have scintillating personalities.

My Tastes

In previous chapters, I have made much of my aesthetic sensitivities, and briefly made reference to things that I happen to like. Perhaps this would be a good place to discuss, in detail, those things that appeal to me in that way. I would like to discuss, in that order, music, art, and literature.

One good way to begin the discussion about music is to list the composers that I consider to be the giants. They are, in chronological order: Bach, Mozart, Beethoven, Wagner, Brahms, Bruckner, and Mahler.

This is not to say that they are the only composers that I enjoy immensely and whose works are well-represented in my collection of recordings. There are many others who, while great, are not in the same league as those. Some even predate Bach (e.g., Monteverdi, Lully, Couperin, and Vivaldi), while others followed Mahler (e.g., Richard Strauss, Korngold, Stravinsky, Elgar, de Falla, and Britten). I even include creators of light fare such as Gilbert and Sullivan, Franz Lehar, and Jacques Offenbach.

If you would bear with me, I would like to give an analogy that would explain this. It is of a geographic nature, and will be immediately understood by anyone who has visited what I consider to be the most beautiful section of the United States: The Pacific Northwest. There is a breathtaking range of mountains called the Cascades. Peaks that rise 10,000 feet are not uncommon. Among these, approximately one hundred miles apart, are a few perennially snow-capped volcanic mountains (ranging from Mt Shasta in the south to Mt Baker in the north) that tower a good 5,000 feet above the Cascades.

Admittedly, most of the 'giants' are from the school of German Romanticism. I am also extremely fond of music from the Renaissance and Baroque periods, though my preference in the Renaissance period is for the sacred[1] rather than the secular. I dismiss the Rococo as the decadence of the Baroque.

---

1   My favorite here is Tomas Luis da Victoria.

Before the age of twelve, I was not particularly interested in music of any kind. Then, one evening, as I turned on the radio, they were playing Siegfried's Funeral Music from Wagner's opera *Die Götterdämmerung*.[2] I was filled by a euphoria unlike anything I had ever before experienced. Not too long after that, I heard the prelude to *Die Meistersinger von Nürnberg*,[3] the first Wagner work I had heard complete. I subscribed to the station's program guide and, as much as possible, listened to every Wagner work they had scheduled.

This was in 1944, and I do not think that I need dwell on the fact that this was not a good year to become a devotee of Wagner. However, at that time, this particular bad opinion of me was, to use a technological metaphor, below the noise level of that sort of thing.

Yet, although I did not realize it at the time, I believe that I had seen things in Wagner that were obscured by the public knowledge that Hitler called him his favorite composer. (Never mind that Hitler also very much enjoyed the operettas of Franz Lehar. Whoever said that guilt by association was rational?) About this more later.

When I was fourteen, a friend of mine played for me his recordings of Jussi Björling. I discovered that there was much to love in the Italian and French repertoire. Not all of it. To this day, I consider everything from Italy between Pergolesi's *La Serva Padrona*[4] and Verdi's *Un Ballo in Maschera*[5] as an operatic wasteland. The main reason is that the music is banal and often tends to trivialize the dramatic situation.

My favorite Italian opera is Puccini's *Turandot*, and my favorite French opera is Debussy's *Pelléas et Mélisande*. This is not to belittle other Italian and French works or composers. Later Verdi is overwhelming.[6] Montemezzi's *L'Amore di Tre Re*[7] is all too seldom performed. The same is true of Massenet's *Manon*, which I like better than the much more popular *Manon Lescaut* of Puccini.[8] Gounod's *Faust* has gorgeous music, but my enthusiasm for that opera is a bit dampened by the fact that his librettists took Goethe's essentially philosophical work and trivialized it into a love

---

2   *The Twilight of the Gods.*

3   *The Mastersingers of Nuremberg.*

4   *The Maid Mistress.*

5   *A Masked Ball.*

6   My favorite is *Otello,* followed closely by *Don Carlo.*

7   *The Love of Three Kings.*

8   I find no small amount of amusement in the stated locale of the final act: the desert outside New Orleans.

story. Goethe's hero wanted enlightenment; Gounod's wanted a potency pill.

Shortly after my introduction to that operatic repertoire, while listening to the radio, I heard the Jascha Heifitz/Arturo Toscanini[9] recording of Beethoven's *Violin Concerto.* By God, I thought, there was great music that did not involve the human voice! I was thus introduced to the purely instrumental repertoire. The first choral work to strike a chord (so to speak) was the Brahms *German Requiem,* which I heard on the radio when I was fifteen.

It has been like an ever-increasing spiral ever since. Even to this day, I am discovering great music that I previously either had not known about or had ignored.

At the age of ten or so they tried to give me piano lessons. At that time I had not yet developed a sensitivity to music, so I was totally unresponsive. They were discontinued. When I did discover music, I wanted to be able to do more than just listen. I still retained knowledge of the piano keyboard and of the basic rudiments of music notation. By myself, I learned to read music and play the piano. (I never was proficient at it because of my poor coordination, but everyone said that I showed good musicianship.)

The way I did it was to take, from the library, musical scores of works with which I was already familiar from listening. This way, knowing how they should sound, I knew when I was making a mistake.

I also would sing, primarily for myself (but also for anyone within earshot), selections from opera, oratorio, and *lieder.* When I was a first year undergraduate student, a friend of mine (who was studying piano at a prestigious New York City music school) told me that he felt that I had a fairly good voice, and that I should train it. I told him that there was no way I could afford voice lessons.

He informed me that the school was awash in scholarship endowment money, and that I should give it a try. He offered to knock on doors to look into it for me. One of my basic beliefs is that, if they say 'no', I am no worse off than if I had not tried. I thanked him and told him to go ahead.

A short while later, he told me that they had scheduled an audition for me, and I was to bring two selections. I brought *Ombra Mai Fu* (commonly known as the *Largo*) from Händel's *Serse,* and *Widmung* (Dedication) by

---

9   The violinist and conductor. I have heard many recordings of this, but my favorite is the one with Joseph Szigeti and Bruno Walter with the New York Philharmonic.

Schumann.[10] I was given a scholarship, and studied voice for three and a half years until I graduated from college and was drafted into the Army.

After that, I did not do much with it, except informally, until 1964, when I was living in Los Angeles, California. A neighbor of mine belonged to a community chorus affiliated with the music department of one of the state colleges. She told me that they were preparing something particularly difficult, and needed singers with some musical sophistication. Thinking that this was a good way to get back into music actively, I went with her. The work involved was Honneger's *King David*. She was right; it was a bear.

After that, wherever I lived, I made it a point to participate in either a concert chorus or a church choir. With the concert choruses, I not only sang the standard chestnuts (*Messiah*, Beethoven's Ninth, the *Requiems* of Mozart and Verdi, and so on), but also works by composers somewhat more out-of-the-way, such as Elgar, Walton, Prokofieff, Britten, and Mahler.

As to church choirs, because the main interest in doing that was musical rather than religious, I restricted myself to groups that sang music that I liked and considered a challenge. The acme was a church in upstate New York. The director was an opera singer with the local regional company. Each Sunday, at the eleven o'clock mass, we sang a mass by Mozart, Haydn, or Schubert. I was totally spoiled; after that, as they say in showbiz, what do you do for an encore?

My tastes in art tend to be somewhat unorthodox. My favorite modern artists are Henry Tanner (a reproduction of his *Annunciation* hangs on a wall in my living room), Jose Orozco, and Salvador Dali.

Also on a living room wall, is a reproduction of Dali's *The Sacrament of the Last Supper*. I think it to be the greatest painting of the twentieth century. (The Tanner painting mentioned before misses that by a couple of years.) All other western *Last Supper* paintings depict the incident when Jesus announces his imminent betrayal, and the ensuing consternation among the disciples. Dali shows the consecration of the bread and wine, which is, in effect, the first mass. (Many Byzantine icons on this subject do the same.)

---

10 For those with an affinity for things romantic, the Schumann song, which has been my audition piece ever since, has an interesting story behind it. Both Schumann, who wrote the music, and Rückert, who wrote the poem, did so as a wedding present for the women they married. Even those who dislike classical music would have to admit that this is better than another toaster.

I find it very interesting that Dali's religious paintings were done after he had become very wealthy from his surrealistic works. My interpretation is that those are what he really wanted to do.

I like Picasso's work from his Blue and Harlequin periods, but, as to the rest of it, I find it pretentious. I liken it to the work of many other trendy modern artists, the adulation of whom gives new meaning to the story of *The Emperor's New Clothes*. One should not interpret this to mean that I like Norman Rockwell. As far as I am concerned, he is the American equivalent of Socialist Realism.

I also much prefer the Baroque to the Renaissance. I find the latter quite bland, while the former vividly depicts the drama that is portrayed. When Renaissance artists painted the Descent from the Cross, according to the facial expressions, they might as well be taking the wash down from the line. Compare that to Rubens' *Descent*. The face of the Madonna shown on Michelangelo's *Pietà* is one of the most beautiful ever, but her expression defies the subject matter. She is holding, in her lap, the body of her son, who has just died a horrible death, yet she seems to be contemplating a bolt of cloth, deciding whether it might make a good slipcover. A comparison of the *David* of Michelangelo and Bernini is also telling. The former looks as though he is posing for his portrait. The latter must be seen, if only in reproduction; it beggars any verbal description.

The Impressionist works are pleasant enough but, to my taste, tend all to look alike. I'm hard put to see where the Expressionist school gets its name. I have read any number of articles attempting to explain this, but, after I finished, not only did I not understand that term, but I could not understand what the commentators had said either.[11] I would call that school Nihilist. I do, though, admire the technical skill of many Expressionist cinema directors, such as Fritz Lang. They managed to get effects that dwarf the computer-generated special effects one sees today.

As to literature, I must call to mind that, while I do have an extensive aesthetic sensitivity, it is with ideas that I have my greatest facility. These are not unrelated, which is why the authors whose ideas impress me the most (even when I disagree with them) are the ones whose works appear to have the greatest beauty of style.

Two writers whose work I enjoy reading, although many of their ideas, while beautifully put, upon analysis can be shown to be rather empty, are

11   This is not limited to art. As a Wagner afficionado, I have vainly attempted to discover, from learned treatises, the significance of the final words of *Parsifal*: 'Erlösung dem Erlöser' ('Salvation to the Savior').

Shaw and Wilde. When I was a college undergraduate, some of my friends told me that some of the answers to my questions about religion could be found in the poetry of Gerard Manley Hopkins.[12] While his style had a beauty to it, I was hard put to glean any ideas directly from reading his works.

There are a number of lionized authors whose supposed genius escapes me totally. Dickens wrote one great novel: *A Tale of Two Cities*. He was supposed to be a great exponent of social reform, but his solution to the poverty problem seems to be: for each poor person, find a rich benefactor or a long-lost rich relative.

Another writer who wrote only one great work was Ibsen: *An Enemy of the People*. In high school, I read *A Doll's House*. When I came to the end, with the door slamming downstairs, my first thought was, 'She'll be back'. The problem addressed was one that is quite serious, but I had a hard time caring for either of the characters; they were so superficial. Dr Stockman was someone about whom one could be greatly concerned.

As for Stendhal and Balzac, they seem to feel that there is no life beyond Parisian high society (or wherever else the locale). This is true about many modern writers also; their characters spend the entire work contemplating their navels and, as such, their problems are essentially self-inflicted.

It is too bad that Jane Austen and the Brontë sisters did not live in this era. They would quite likely have made a great deal of money by writing movie scripts for the *Lifetime* TV network.

I have generally found most fiction, as such, boring. One noteworthy exception was *Dracula*. I cannot understand why every motion picture made, using that title, did not simply do a straight adaptation of Stoker's novel. They all suffer as a result.

Another novel that has been ill-served on the screen is *Frankenstein*. In Shelley's book, the creature (I cannot call him a monster) is not a brute who, unmindful of his strength, kills at random. He is very articulate and sensitive, and focuses his anger on the one responsible for creating him into a world in which he is abhorred.

It is significant that Victor Frankenstein is not killed until the very end; the creature first kills those dear to his creator. When I read it, I could not help but think of Milton's Satan in *Paradise Lost*, who tried to revenge himself on God by attacking the new race of humans, whom God loved.

12   He was a convert to Catholicism who became a Jesuit priest.

I greatly enjoyed Graham Greene's *The Power and the Glory* because it had, for me, an interesting thesis. It was that a good cause (the Catholic faith) can be served by a person (the priest) with bad intentions (his pride). Likewise, a bad cause (the revolution, which was as oppressive as the dictatorship it overthrew) can be served by a person (the police officer) with good intentions (the people would ultimately have a better life because of what he did). This did not prevent the good cause from being good, as I read the ending.

I discussed music before, but, in the case of opera,[13] there are plots and characters involved, so it can also be discussed as literature. I should first like to mention two operas, each of which contains a leading character that I find so distasteful, that he or she negates the effect of whatever good music the composer created.

One is *Pique Dame*[14] by Tchaikovsky. The character in question is Lisa, who throws away the love of Prince Yeletsky, a high-ranking nobleman who is good and kind, for Gherman, a totally worthless gambler. She commits suicide (after singing a *bravura* aria) when she believes herself to have been deserted by Gherman.

Massenet wrote some of his best music for *Werther,* yet the title character is one with whom I cannot sympathize. He becomes obsessed with Charlotte, who has allowed the dead hand of her mother to dictate her life to her, against her own wishes. (That has to mean trouble.) For this, he ignores the interest shown in him by Charlotte's younger sister, who seems to be just what the doctor would have ordered for his *angst* and *ennui.* After Charlotte's marriage to Albert, he continues to press his suit, which has to make her, at the very least, uncomfortable. Lastly, he arranges his suicide so that Charlotte will be with him, leaving her a lifetime legacy of guilt.

There are only two comments to be made about this opera. One is that saddling Charlotte with discomfort and guilt is, at the very least, a strange way of demonstrating one's love. The other is that Albert has to be the most patient and understanding man in all fiction. It may be the essence of cynicism to say that this is why Charlotte preferred Werther to Albert, but there is something in the background of another opera, Puccini's *La Bohème*, that tends to support this thesis. The source of this opera is a novel

---

13   The same can be said to be true of oratorio, of which I am also quite fond, but I should like to consider only opera.

14   *The Queen of Spades.*

by Henri Murger: *Scènes de la Vie de Bohème.*[15] In it, he states that Musette, among all the men she had known, loved Marcel alone, because he was the only man who could make her suffer.

In spite of the title character, the music that Massenet wrote for *Werther* makes listening to that opera an enjoyable experience. There are some other cases for which the greatness of the music overcomes texts that range from the laughable to the objectionable. A prime case in point is *Dido and Æneas* of Purcell. Another is Beethoven's *Fidelio,* which is one of my favorites. Forcing oneself to read the text, without hearing Beethoven's music, is a good way to build character. The text of Mendelssohn's *Elijah* portrays God as someone who might be auditioning for the part of a third character in the film *Grumpy Old Men.*

Earlier, I gave Wagner as an example of a creative artist whose personal life and philosophical writings belied the ideas in his artistic creations. (This can be seen directly, since he chose his stories and wrote his own libretti.) I have described his personal life. His philosophical writings are anti-Jewish. (Yet, for the premiere of *Parsifal,* he chose a Jewish conductor, Hermann Levi.) They are also ultra-nationalist to the point of jingoism. The ideas in his musical creations seem to come not from just another person, but from another galaxy.

In *Der Fliegender Holländer* and *Tannhäuser,* the heroes are released from the curses they brought on themselves through the self-sacrifice of the heroines. (The real Wagner acted as though the highest calling anyone could possibly have was to sacrifice themselves for him.) In *Der Ring des Nibelungen,*[16] the theme is that love and greed are mutually exclusive; the one could be had only if the other were renounced. (The real Wagner's lust and greed were boundless.)

In *Die Meistersinger von Nürnberg,*[17] there were three instances in which Wagner the composer and Wagner the person could not recognize one another. In an Act II monologue, Hans Sachs is thinking about an unusual song he heard that morning. He meditates that, while the song may have broken established rules, there must be other rules that apply to it; one must not break rules without others to replace them. (The real Wagner

15   *Scenes from the Bohemian Life.*

16   *The Ring of the Nibelung,* a series of four operas with a continuing story line (an operatic miniseries?), taken from German, Norse, and Icelandic mythology. They are *Das Rheingold (The Rhinegold), Die Walküre (The Valkyrie), Siegfried,* and *Die Götterdämmerung (The Twilight of the Gods).*

17   *The Mastersingers of Nuremberg.*

refused to consider that any rules, at any time, could apply to him.) Sachs renounces his love for the young Eva because he knows it to be the right and wise thing to do. (The real Wagner never renounced anything, least of all the love of his benefactors' wives.)

At the end of the opera, Sachs delivers an admonition that the real glory and endurance of a nation lay not in its military or imperial power, but in the honor that people give to their native artists. This ideological theme must have gone right over Hitler's head.

The same is true about the *Ring*. When Hitler talked about the end of his Third Reich, it was in terms of going out in a blaze of glory, like the gods at the end of the *Ring*. The fact of the matter is, if one studies those operas, the gods were justly destroyed because of their greed.

In *Boris Godunov* (another favorite of mine, with a libretto written by Mussorgsky, the composer), the tragedy of the Russian people is that, in their desire for someone to deliver them from their misery, they flock to a deliverer who turns out to be a worse tyrant than the last one. And this was Stalin's favorite opera?

I should like to close this chapter by stating that I often find myself in sympathy with characters that the author, I have to admit, did not intend to portray as sympathetic. In fact, the author, I would imagine, would have wanted the reader to consider them as worthy of being outcasts. They are usually cast as the villains. One notable exception to this would be the very sympathetic heroes of Benjamin Britten's operas. Consider, for example, Peter Grimes, Albert Herring, Billy Budd, and Owen Wingrave, all of whom are oddballs if not outcasts.

In Shakespeare's *King Lear*, I developed an immediate fondness for Edmund, the illegitimate son of the Duke of Gloucester, after hearing, at the beginning, his father's conversation about him with the Earl of Kent.[18] Later in the play, when Edmund has his father's eyes gouged out, I could not, in spite of the gruesomeness of it, get over the feeling that the old man had it coming.

Someone who, it appears, is easy to villainize is a husband[19] who is portrayed as 'cold' and 'distant'. He is, nevertheless, a man who works hard to provide for his wife and is genuinely concerned for her welfare. He does

18   'Though this knave came into the world before he was sent for, yet was his mother fair. There was good sport at his making, and the whoreson must be acknowledged.'

19   Or wife, as the case might be. Consider Ethan Frome's wife, with whom I sympathized when we read the novel of that name in high school, much to the bewilderment of the teacher and my classmates.

not, though, provide any 'excitement' or 'fulfillment'. She gets involved with a man who does provide those, but for whom she is essentially a toy and who suddenly is no longer available when the situation becomes too complicated for his taste. Conceivably she could return to her husband a sadder but wiser woman (as the wife does in Hitchcock's film *I Confess*), but instead does something totally irrational. Is this not the plot of Tolstoy's *Anna Karenina*? I have long since come to the belief that the search for fulfillment is a luxury that can only be indulged by those who have totally conquered the problem of survival. Most people in the world have not.

Another husband who, when I read the book, won my sympathy was that of Constance Chatterley. According to the author, her husband was unable to perform sexually because of wounds suffered in combat service during wartime. Most husbands, in such a situation (from what I have seen and read), would have become consumed with jealousy if they saw their wives in innocent conversation with another man. Lord Chatterley, wanting to maintain everything in his marriage that did not involve sex, gave her his blessing to seek a physical outlet elsewhere. When she got totally involved, emotionally and otherwise, with that clod Mellors, I thought that her husband's anger was totally justified. In this book, Lawrence portrays women as being totally in thrall to their emotions, devoid of any reason whatsoever. This would make them not to be trusted with any serious decision-making. Is this view not sexist?

I realize that I have viewed the characters I mentioned in terms of what their actions should have been had they been logical, but that is the only way I know of how to view the world. Yet, the thing that makes for drama is irrational behavior (just as incongruousness and ambiguity are the things that make for humor). Had Oedipus acted rationally, he would have concluded that a confrontation with this cantankerous old man was scarcely worth his bother and granted him the right-of-way. Had that happened, would Sophocles' play have become a classic, or would his name have been given to that complex?

One example of my idea of a sympathetic character is bound to stir some controversy initially. It is Stanley Kowalski in Tennessee Williams' *A Streetcar Named Desire*.[20] I had never seen Marlon Brando's stage portrayal at the time that I read the play (which, it seems to me, has an ending quite different from the film version), so all I had to go with was the text itself.

---

20   It contains, in my opinion, the only good line Williams wrote: 'I've always depended on the kindness of strangers.'

Far from the disgusting brute of popular opinion, I saw someone who was articulate and rather knowledgeable, and who had the perspicacity to see Blanche as a manipulative phony who feeds her ego regardless of how others may be affected.

Of course, while I can understand why he was so angry with her, that in no way excuses what he did to her. There are less draconian ways he could have dealt with that.

In Leoncavallo's opera *I Pagliacci*,[21] Canio kills Nedda, his wife, and Silvio, her 'suitor'.[22] She could so easily have saved her life and gone off with Silvio. After venting his rage at her, he tells her to leave, that she is not worthy of his grief.[23] She cannot resist tormenting him further.

I have saved for the last, my choice for the most sympathetic character in Wagner's *Ring*. It is Alberich, the Nibelung dwarf. Why?

This could be considered a strange choice. If one looks at the text, he is meanspirited and vengeful, and, with the exception of The Curse on the Ring, his music contains not one whistleable tune.

To explain this seemingly strange choice, I must discuss my thoughts about 'teasing'. I define it as holding in someone's view something that person wants a great deal, but purposely withholding it, causing that person to suffer. A synonym is 'tantalize', which comes from the story of Tantalus.[24] The gods thought this a fit punishment for someone who had done an evil thing, yet teasing is often done to someone who has done the teaser no harm, and is usually done solely for ego-enhancement. I see this as nothing but gratuitous cruelty.

Is this not what the Rhine Daughters did to Alberich? When, after they finish teasing him, he hears from them the secret of the gold, and is told that a ring forged from it brings its power only to those who renounce love, he decides that, if he cannot have love, at least he can have power. Later, when Wotan[25] steals the gold ring from him (to pay for an ill-advised project), he finds himself deprived of both love and power.

Wagner depicted Alberich as repulsive, both physically and musically. Yet, when the final curtain goes down on the *Ring*, the only main

---

21   *The Clowns.*

22   I hate to use any version of the word 'love' in this context.

23   'Va, non meriti il mio duol!'

24   In Greek mythology, he was a king who revealed the secrets of the gods. After his death, he was punished eternally by being placed in water up to his chin and under a fruit tree just within his grasp. These receded whenever he tried to assuage his thirst or hunger.

25   The king of the gods.

characters left alive are Alberich and the Rhine Daughters. I have to wonder if Wagner did not send a message there.

A good way to end this topic is with my thoughts on criticism. (Never mind that, here, I have indulged in lots of it.) I believe that one should not read commentary or criticism on the arts until one has familiarized oneself with the works themselves. This should be preceded, as I did, by studying the forms and techniques used in the arts so that the message can be more fully appreciated by knowledge of the medium.

What I am referring to here are the interpretations that are put on works of art by critics who seem to bring too much of their own baggage into what they do. A good work of art is usually well-focused, and such critics tend to obscure rather than clarify. There are two good examples.

Aside from Debussy's music, a major appeal, for me, of *Pelléas et Mélisande* is the dreamlike quality and unresolved questions of Maeterlinck's play (which formed the libretto). I find it difficult to see how anyone approaching it, with the Freudian baggage that some critics have heaped on it, can fail to miss these qualities.

I have already written of the points Wagner was trying to make in his music dramas. They are totally blurred by the Marxist interpretations of George Bernard Shaw, and others. This is not to say that a critic does not have good ideas. I enjoy reading the reviews and essays of Eduard Hanslick, who loathed Wagner.

My favorite artist's rejoinder to a critic was given by Salvador Dali. When he produced, for the second time, a painting that contained an elephant with spindly legs, a critic accused him of 'a lazy reliance on symbols he has used before'. Dali's rejoinder: 'Look at Raphael. Madonnas, madonnas, madonnas.'

When I was an undergraduate, I was discussing something with a professor whose specialty was medieval history. Another student came by and, after joining the conversation, asked what was a good book to read to find out about St Paul. The professor said, 'Why don't you read his letters?'

What I Mean by the Word 'Love'

Perhaps a digression is in order here to discuss just what, to me, is meant by 'love', and the extent, if any, to which I am capable of experiencing it. This is important because of an incident that occurred at the age of fourteen. I was giving vent to the usual teenage *angst*. At one point my mother, exasperated at me, said, 'You know what the trouble with you is? You don't know how to love! You need to learn how to love!' I was taken aback totally. I hadn't the faintest notion what she meant. I still don't.

It is commonly said that languages derived from Latin (i.e., French, Spanish, or Italian; I know almost nothing of Portuguese or Romanian) are the best in which to discuss love. I think that this is nonsense. How can you operate in a language which makes no distinction between 'love' and 'like'? How is a woman supposed to know whether you want to marry her or just be a good buddy?

Languages such as English and German do make such a distinction, but, to discuss love, my favorite language is Greek. They have three words: φίλος *(philos),* αγάπη *(agape), and* έρος *(eros).* Their meanings can be summed up as: love from the head, love from the heart, and love from the sex hormones. Looking back, the only one of which I was ever capable was *philos.* For all of my life, even when I came to be quite fond of someone, it was an intellectual appreciation of that person rather than one that was 'heartfelt'.

It is interesting to note that, when St Paul wrote his eloquent discourse on love in I Corinthians 13, the word that he used was *agape.*[1]

On the subject of different types of love, *eros* should be addressed. The only way I have ever felt sexual arousal is through fantasy. The only attraction I feel for an actual woman is as an aesthetic object, not a

---

[1] One disclaimer that is in order here is that words like 'heart', as pertaining to emotion, are purely metaphoric. The use of these words, in this context, goes back to Aristotle's notion of the heart being the seat of the emotions. Today, we know that the only thing that the heart does is pump blood, and that the emotions, like the intellect, reside in the brain.

hormonally sexual one. (To anticipate the obvious question, I am *not* gay; the male body has no attraction for me of any kind.)

Even so, for me, no appreciation of a woman, personal or otherwise, has ever so much as gotten started if I did not find her willing and able to join me in an intelligent conversation. This has always been the initial stimulation, and without it no interest in her was even begun.

I had a recent experience that illustrates this notion of arousal only through fantasy. I was riding public transportation, and across from me sat a young woman who was not unattractive. She wore a short, flared dress and sat in such a way that I could not help but see *everything*. (Any further details than that are unnecessary.) The only amusement I got out of that was in seeing something I was not supposed to see. I felt no arousal, in the sense of any desire to have sexual relations with her or even to approach her. On the other hand, at any time since then, when I have thought about that incident, I *have* felt sexually aroused.

Looking back, I do not think that I have ever experienced a genuine physical orgasm. The best thing I have ever had to accompany an ejaculation is what I call a 'neurological jolt' which is invariably followed by an immediate letdown. I use the modifier 'physical' because I have had experiences that I consider must be the equivalent of such a sensation. However, they are only of two types. One is aesthetic (such as from a superb performance of a great piece of music, a great work of art, or a beautifully written passage in literature). The other is intellectual (such as coming across the expression of an idea – my own or someone else's – that ties together a bunch of loose ends).

The foregoing presupposes that the physical orgasm is neither overrated nor has been oversold. (How do you measure pleasure; or, for that matter, pain?) The intellectual and aesthetic pleasures that I have had could very well be beggared by others that I have never experienced. One possibility is the spiritual. As evidence of this, all one need do is to look at the facial expression on Bernini's magnificent sculpture *The Ecstasy of St Teresa*.

This is not to say that I have never had a pleasurable experience with a real woman whom I have found to be attractive, in the sense I have described above. It is just that, as I now recall, in order for the experience to be pleasurable, I had to invent a rather interesting mechanism, in other words, aesthetic fantasizing about her during that time.

In discussing 'love', one hears a great deal about having a 'relationship'. Currently, when one uses that word (which I use at times), it is taken to mean one is having sex exclusively with one other person – for the time being. I tend to the more traditional definition: any interaction between two people. This can range from a casual acquaintance to a committed marriage.

A Missing Faculty

In his book *An Anthropologist On Mars,*[1] Oliver Sacks tells of a man who had been blind for decades. That man had developed his other senses, particularly hearing and touch, so as to be able to function quite well. Analogously, I seem to have compensated (some say I have over-compensated) for my emotional deficit by developing my intellectual and aesthetic sensibilities. By some newly-discovered medical technique, the man's sight was restored, with surprising results. Far from adding to his sensory faculties, the balance that the man had developed among the senses that had been left him after loss of his sight was destroyed, to the point where he was quite disoriented psychologically.

It makes me wonder whether or not I would even want to be given the capability to feel the emotions others feel if my other faculties were to suffer as a result.

On this topic of compensating, there was something that happened to me, in another context, when I got out of the hospital after those electric shock treatments. They are quite notorious for impairing short-term memory. I had wanted to resume my normal activities as soon as possible, so I rejoined my church choir on the following Sunday. The music was our usual repertoire, but I could swear that I had never seen it before. Amazingly, I discovered that I could sing it at sight! Shortly after that, my memory did recover, but I have retained that sight-reading ability to this day.

As a digression, it has long been a belief of mine that one should beware of asking God for a physical miracle; He might just give it to you to show you how ill-considered your request was. In Eugen d'Albert's opera *Die Todten Augen*[2] the heroine, who has been blind for most of her life, is the wife of the Roman governor of Jerusalem at the time of Jesus Christ's earthly ministry. She loves her husband dearly, but is tormented by the fact that she has never been able to see what he looks like.

1   Sacks, Oliver(1995) *An Anthropologist On Mars.* New York: Knopf.
2   *The Dead Eyes.*

When she hears of Jesus' entry into the city, and of the miracles that He has performed, she asks to be taken to Him and asks Him to restore her sight. When He does so, she is overjoyed and rushes to see her husband, only to find that he is unspeakably ugly. She spends a whole day staring at the sun so that she can be blind once more.

As I said, I digress.

Why should I not want such a restoration of emotions to take place? It could certainly be asked: wouldn't such a reestablishment of the 'connecting' emotions enable me to relate to people in a way that I now cannot? The fact of the matter is that I do relate right now, but in a manner different from that of the NT ('neurologically-typical'), just as the blind man manages to function in his environment differently from the sighted.

(I will continue to use this analogy because I find it quite to the point; the blind man is missing a very important physical faculty possessed by most people, while I am missing a psychological one. When I say 'missing faculty' instead of 'disability' it is *not* a euphemism, but a deliberate choice of words, even though, in a strictly technical sense, it is a disability.)

Later on, I should like to relate this phenomenon (of doing things differently than the NT) to two items. One is my religious beliefs and my social conscience (these two are, for me, totally interdependent). The other is the question of any ability I might be able to have to form a rewarding relationship with a woman. On that last item, the analogy of the blind man will figure quite prominently.

Two Perilous Characteristics

There are two symptoms of autism that have also played a prominent rôle in my life: having a very high pain threshold and being blasé about physical dangers. (The fear emotion of which I wrote earlier concerns itself only with uncertainty about the future and unwanted intrusion into the space I have staked out for myself.) I am convinced that, when I was in the Army, if I had gone into combat situations, I would have returned either with a chest full of decorations or in a body bag.

There is an incident that occurred in the summer of 1968 that illustrates this. I had locked myself out of my house. I realized that the only way I was going to get back in was to break a small window on my front door so that I could unlock that door from the inside. I could have looked about for a rock or some other such thing. I did not; I only took note of the fact that the heel of my hand was right there. Without thinking at all of the possible danger involved, I shoved the heel of my hand through that pane of glass.

Predictably, a piece of that broken glass sliced everything on my forearm all the way to the bone. To the point, I felt nothing, and did not realize that I'd been injured until I glanced down and saw the open, gaping wound and the blood that had gushed all over the front door. Even then, I felt neither fear nor panic.

It might also be mentioned that, in recent years, I have undergone two hernia repair operations. The procedure is not complicated but requires an ostensibly painful recovery, to the point of rendering one immobile. Looking back, I was immobilized, not from severe pain (it could have been called extreme discomfort), but from fear that movement might tear the stitches. That fear was totally unfounded, as my surgeon reassured me when I repeatedly called him about feeling them tear.

Can 'Heartless' Pity be Real?

For all of my adolescent and adult life, I have been socially conscious, advocating equality and help for the poor and disadvantaged. Yet looking back, I now realize that this was something born out of an intellectual conviction that this was morally right, rather than an identification with the people I was trying to help.

People tend to dismiss a logical approach to social and economic problems, claiming that, being 'unfeeling', it has to lead to self-interest. An example is: if one is hungry, it would be logical to steal food from someone else who has it. However, a powerful factor mitigating against that sort of thing is an intellectual appreciation of the difference between right and wrong. This would be unencumbered by emotional factors such as pride, greed, or envy, which certainly promote such self-interest.

Everyone is familiar with the expression, 'I can feel for you, but I can't quite reach you'. The former is all I am capable of. The German word for 'pity' is *mitleid*, which literally means 'suffer with'. (The same goes for the words 'compassion' and 'sympathy'. The only difference is that the former has Latin roots, while the latter's are Greek.)

A beautiful application of *mitleid* is given in Wagner's opera *Parsifal*. A community of knights is suffering because of a curse placed on their king due to a sin he committed (a curse that is accompanied by a painful wound that will not heal). They receive a prophesy that a naïve ignoramus will gain wisdom and enlightenment through pity for the king's suffering and will both heal the wound and redeem him from the curse.

When such a one shows up in the knights' realm, he witnesses the king's agony, but is unmoved. It is only later, when he actually feels the king's pain in his own flesh that he gains this wisdom and enlightenment. He returns to redeem the king from his curse and heal his wound.

Again, I can deeply appreciate all of this as I listen to this opera, but not in my day-to-day life with people. I must rely on that intellectual appreciation.

There is no small irony in that fact that, when I was once asked to say a short prayer in a Catholic service, part of what I said was, '...for those who, in this life, have been blessed with comfort and affluence; that in the suffering of the poor they may see the suffering of Christ, and that in the victims of injustice they may see the injustice of the Crucifixion...' I have never seen any such things; it was always intellectual with me. Even those words came, not from any inner intuitive experience, but from aesthetic creativity. They did, though, mirror my ideas.

Grief

Love, in the *agape* sense, is not the only emotion for which I seem to have no capacity. One rather fundamental emotion felt by people is grief when someone close is lost, either through death or permanent departure for a far-off place. Never in my life have I ever felt grief, or even a sense of loss.

This was brought out in very high relief to me when my mother died in October of 1994. My brother was devastated, even though we all saw her death coming. (He and I had even worked on the list of 'things to do' and on her obituary before she actually died; it was that imminent, but it did not occur precipitously.) Everyone else in the family, and friends also, expressed sorrow.

I felt nothing. I also felt that there was something wrong there. Somewhat sardonically, I said to my pastor (who had been a psychologist before becoming a priest), 'There are all kinds of support groups for people who grieve, but nothing for people who should be grieving but don't'.

This was before I even dreamed of myself as being autistic. When I read the remark, quoted in the *New Yorker* article 'Prodigies' by Oliver Sacks, of that 15-year-old boy who had just lost his mother (January 9, 1995, page 51, last column), I searched back as far as I could remember, even to early childhood, and noted that my reaction to my mother's death was no isolated case.

It was not limited to family members, but also to close friends. There were two people who went out of their way to help me when I was in dire straits. They had no obligation to help me and, in some ways, could have caused problems for themselves by doing so. I remember feeling no pain of loss when told of their deaths (in one case, it was quite sudden and he was young). Any sorrow I felt was purely intellectual.

In March of 1996, spent some time, in solitude, at my daughter's home, taking care of her house and her cat while she and her family were on vacation. (The cat and I became good buddies.) My daughter had just had to have her other cat euthanized. That remaining cat was obviously grieving for her longtime companion. I could not help but think that a cat, the most independent of God's creatures, can grieve, but I cannot.

I am, though, able to intellectually appreciate the grief of another. At one time, I saw an old man lamenting the recent death of his wife. I thought about how there must have been a great deal of love to produce that much grief. Not being able to feel what he felt, I was at a total loss as to what to say to him. But, then, so was everybody else.

The irony of this is that I can get all weepy at the tear-jerker endings of operas such as *La Traviata*, *La Bohème*, or *Madama Butterfly*, or novels such as *Dracula*. (Yes, I actually *have* read that book.) Yet, as noted above, I feel nothing in real-life emotional situations. This is connected with that topic of feeling 'emotion' only through art.

This is a good place to reiterate that these emotions, as expressed through the arts, consist of sights, sounds, and words. They register on the intellectual and aesthetic sensibilities. Real-life emotions appear to me to consist of things felt in an unexpressed manner, and with another person also feeling them, almost in the manner of sympathetic vibrations at a resonant frequency.

There is, in the third act of Puccini's opera *Turandot*, a beautiful phrase about unexpressed feelings, when the slave girl Liú, just before her suicide, sings about 'So much love, secret and unconfessed.'[1]

---

1   'Tanto amore, segreto ed inconfessato.'

Death and the Afterlife

Since grief is so often associated with someone's death, and the sense of loss that accompanies it, this would be a good place for me to discuss my ideas on the subject. The sense of loss is usually associated with the question of what, if anything, has happened to the one who was lost.

Note that, in the chapter title, I did not use quote marks. That is an indication that I do believe in an afterlife. Why?

I would like to start with a story about my first contact with the concept of death, at the age of four or five. It shows not only my reaction to how this was initially presented to me, but also a quality I possessed, even at that age, which enabled me, in later life, to have a facility with advanced mathematics.

Someone in my family, quite elderly, had just died. I found the ensuing consternation on everyone's part very discomforting. That was, mostly, because I did not know what it was that caused this climate of great agitation. (Remember that I wrote that uncertainty was my biggest source of fear.)

When I asked my maternal grandmother what had happened, she told me that so-and-so had died. I asked her what she meant by that. Her reply, in order to be understood, has to be considered in the context that the family in which I grew up were all dyed-in-the-wool atheists.

Her explanation was one of total finality to one's being. This included any consciousness of one's own existence. When I asked her why that had to be, she replied, 'When a shoe gets so old that you can't wear it anymore, you have to throw it in the garbage.'

I remember thinking that she had, at best, used a poor analogy; her conclusion did not necessarily follow from her premise. The shoe could be kept on a shelf or in a dresser drawer. It did not have to be discarded. Thus, it was not this awful notion of death that disturbed me (that did not disturb me at all). It was her bad logic.

Before I go on, definitions are in order. 'Death' occurs when the laws of biology and chemistry come together to cause cessation of all functions of the body. (Given that, everyone has to die sometime of something.)

'Afterlife' means that there is a part of one's essence that survives death, and that this includes a continued consciousness of one's existence.

In that sense, do I believe in an afterlife? Yes, I do. Why?

My belief in the existence of a supreme intelligence (or, if you will, a God) is based on scientific factors. Physicists are devoting a great deal of effort to finding the age of the universe. One does not invest that kind of effort to find an infinite number. The fact that this would be a finite number presupposes that the universe had to have a beginning. (I could use the 'C' word – 'creation', but that puts many people off.) My own graduate study in physics supports this contention.

That being the case, would there be a component to each human being that might survive physical death? (For brevity, I use the 'S' word: 'soul'.) The question of an afterlife is the question of the immortality of that soul upon the death of the body.

Humans are the only animals with the ability to ponder the meaning of their existence. Given that it was whoever, or whatever, created humans gave them this ability, I am hard put to believe that the insights garnered in this process should pass into nothingness upon physical death.

(I realize that this reasoning involves coming to a conclusion by elimination of all known possibilities, except for one. Those in the natural sciences do that all the time. In mathematics, on the other hand, one must rigorously prove that all possibilities have been considered. Admittedly, I have not done that.)

Now I would like to get into some bad logic that I have observed on the subject of immortality. It involves both believers and nonbelievers.

If one believes in an afterlife, especially in the Christian context, then, if one has tried to be as good as possible in this life, death is a transition to something immeasurably better. All the terrible things that happen to one in this life are as if they had never happened.

If that is the case, why are they so terrified of death? Why do they wish each and all long life? (They obviously mean this life. Isn't eternal life rather long?) And, when someone has died, why do they carry on as though that person has gone to ultimate destruction?

And why should they be supporters of capital punishment? Is that not saying, in effect, that termination of one's physical being is the worst punishment that can be inflicted? Given their supposed belief in an afterlife, executing someone, who has had opportunity to repent his or her misdeeds, is actually bestowing the greatest reward, not inflicting the worst penalty.

Hamlet recognized as much when he refrained from killing his uncle while the latter was praying, saying that sending his father's murderer to Heaven was poor revenge indeed.[1]

Is it that, for all their talk of an afterlife, they, in their heart of hearts, really believe in the finality of death? Also, does not this feed the propaganda of the antireligious, that talk of an afterlife is so much whistling in the dark?

Now, what of those who claim there is no such thing? What bad logic have I seen there? Just as those who claim to believe in an afterlife act as though there really isn't one, those who deny its existence often behave as though there might be one after all. They go through incredible intellectual gyrations to insist on some sort of 'immortality'. In looking at these, one must keep in mind that there is no real immortality without a continuing consciousness of one's own existence.

They talk of achieving immortality through one's offspring. Here they lose sight (if they ever had it) that each of one's children has a will and intellect totally independent from that of the parent. He or she is a completely new person with a new existence and essence. Coupled with this is a totally independent consciousness, in which no one else is able to partake.

Thus, one cannot achieve immortality through one's children any more than can a childless person. For those familiar with Strindberg's play *The Father*, the wife of the title character uses this notion of immortality to torture and drive him mad, by hinting that their only child is not his. In one scene, he actually does beg her not to deprive him of his immortality by telling him that.

They also talk about having immortality through the remembrance of others. Does this imply that a homeless person, who dies without family or friends, has no immortality?

Relative to this is people giving sums of money to establish lasting things that will bear their name. They want to 'live on' in these bequests, by having their names noted, even by those who never knew or even heard of them. People will continue to note their names, but, without any continued consciousness, they are totally oblivious to it, and are no better off than one who does not leave a monument. There is an interesting aside to having one's name 'remembered'. Among those mentioned by name in the New Testament are Pontius Pilate, Judas Iscariot, the two Herods, and

1   Act III, Scene 3.

Caiaphas. On the other hand, there are others who are known only as the good Samaritan, the centurion, the good thief, the Samaritan woman, and Pilate's wife.

The urge to have one's name enshrined after one's demise also appears in people's desire for fancy funerals and formal displays of grief. If, as the nonbelievers claim, death is a total finality, one is not going to be aware of any ceremony or lack of it.

The desire for those formal displays of grief brings up another question: why do people measure the sincerity and commitment of another's love by the extent that the other person can be made to suffer? I always think of Shakespeare's sonnet 71.[2] (It must be read in its entirety; it cannot be paraphrased.) That, to me, represents real love and concern for those left behind after one's death.

There is also the notion, that I have heard from many sources, that one can live on through one's ideas. Most people in the world work hard all their lives, with little to show for it except survival. They do not have the luxury of developing ideas. Have they no immortality?

Finally, there is something fascinating I have noticed in many people who are not simply nonreligious, but antireligious. I have seen them make their friends and relatives swear that, after their death, there will be no prayers or other religious observations for them. As if, given their belief, they would in any way know whether or not those promises were really kept.

Those who claim there is an afterlife behave as though there is not, and those who deny its existence act as though there is one. Am I missing something?

2   The opening line reads: 'No longer mourn for me when I am dead.'

Solitude and Loneliness

In addition to never feeling grief, I have never felt lonely or a need for what could be called 'the warmth of another human being', even a loving woman, or a good friend of either sex. I have very much enjoyed the company of those with whom I could have an interesting and stimulating conversation, but not, as so many other people seem to be able to do, simply because he or she is 'a good person' (even though, while tongue-tied in such a social situation, I am able to greatly appreciate this quality as so-called frosting on the cake for those with whom I can relate). Yet, with people who fervently share interests with me, I have been able to form very close friendships.

This trait of never being lonely actually goes deeper than that. Every person, I am told, is capable of retreating inside himself or herself, and shutting the world out, especially when confronted by a stressful environment. I live like that all the time, in good times as well as bad.

In connection with this, I have always been able, when needed, to maintain solitude, even in the midst of a large crowd of people. Others, when they want to 'get away from it all', have to go to some place that is uninhabited, or nearly so. I am able to do that wherever I am.

This shutting-out, though, is not done via an impenetrable barrier, but by what might be called a semipermeable membrane.

As such, I have never felt what could be called an emotional void that needed to be filled by another person, nor do I possess anything with which someone else's emotional void could be filled. I have always known that I fit the usual pattern of the kind of person who could be called a 'loner', but, until recently, I have not been able even to conceive of the depth of that.

Learning

This penchant for solitude manifested itself even when I started school. My teachers were at a total loss to explain why it was that, although I appeared to do no work in the classroom (because I did not interact with my classroom environment), tests showed that I had both absorbed and mastered the material.

Later on, when I was in the fifth grade, the school authorities wanted, as an example to the other kids, to set me back a couple of grades because I did not do any of the classroom work (even though, as earlier, I showed proficiency in the material). My mother preempted this by taking me for evaluation at New York University. (This was in 1942, before autism was first diagnosed. I seem to have had hard luck with that sort of thing.)

I tested as quite gifted, and the people at NYU recommended to my school that I should actually be advanced a grade or two because the work in my current grade was too simple for me.

The only compromise that the school would make was not to set me back, because advancement would have set a bad example.

If I did not do the work in class, how did I learn? Furthermore, how do I still continue to learn? Many people that know me have referred to me by the great compliment of 'walking encyclopedia', and ask me how I learned so much. The answer that I usually give is, 'I read a lot'. But, the fact of the matter is, I *do not*. Because of my attention deficit, I actually read very little. I find, though, that I am able to absorb, retain, and digest more information from an article than I do from a book.

It does help that I have a love of learning. I could even call it a voracious appetite. I am hard put to think of a single course that I took, in either high school or beyond, in which I did not use the knowledge gotten there as a foundation for building further knowledge on my own. Yet, this would do me little good if I were not able to absorb this learning.

To explain this seeming paradox, I considered an analogy between the human thinking process and a computer. The brain can be considered to be like the storage and the processor. Data for the computer to store and process must somehow be fed in via communication channels to the outside world. I liken these communication channels to the learning process.

Most autistic people have severe communication difficulties. This would indicate that they do not have the kind of communication channels possessed by most people, which is why they demonstrate learning difficulties when taught by conventional methods. It may be that autistic *savants* and high functioning autistics have extraordinary channels. (*Extra* is the Latin preposition for 'outside'. As a result, that word 'extraordinary' must be taken in the literal sense: 'outside' the ordinary.)

I get the impression that little study has been done on this. Consequently, having only this smallest intuitive grasp of how I learn, I am extremely hard put to explain the process to others. I have suggested this hypothesis (of extraordinary communication channels) to a number of professionals in the field. One did tell me that this approach is being taken with a view to explaining parapsychology.

In light of this, those who previously thought of me as mysterious might now consider me spooky.

Considering that, in many ways (personal relationships excluded), I have been successful, I would have had to break out of that pattern of self-isolation somewhere in school. This happened in my sophomore year in high school. Before that, while I was able to learn, in my own way, I never really related to schoolwork. This was even true of 'mathematics'. The quotation marks are deliberate. In those days, it consisted of endless drilling in arithmetic calculations. I hated it, because I had understood what needed to be done, and was able to master the methods after working out a couple of examples.[1]

In the year mentioned, I studied plane geometry. Here, instead of rote mechanical operations, I had come to deal with such things as universal and abstract principles, proof construction, and deductive logic.

I loved it! I wanted to get deeply involved in the subject matter, and that made me also want to do the same in other subjects, in the arts and humanities, as well as in mathematics and the sciences. From that point on, I was able to shine in school, at all levels.

I wrote earlier of a 'love of learning', and should like to go into what that all means to me. It is not just a phrase.

---

[1]   Ironically, prior to the invention, in the ninth century, of 'arabic' numbers, there was no notation with which calculations could be done. This did not seem to trouble those who designed and built the architecture of ancient Egypt, Greece, Rome, and the early Middle Ages.

In popular psychology, we are urged to 'get in touch with our inner child'. The Bible says we cannot enter Heaven unless we come as little children.[2] What does all this mean?

When people say 'childlike', they often mean trusting, almost to the point of gullibility. People would like a world in which they could trust others (a wish essentially nullified by their penchant for surreptitiousness). Many in business, in the churches, in schools, and in government would certainly like to encourage this.

But children, ideally, live in an environment in which their more worldly elders protect them from the consequences of undeserved trust. They will not always be able to do so. In addition, Jesus did warn people to 'beware of false prophets'.[3] St Paul[4] wrote that he stopped acting like a child when he became an adult. So, the prudent adult person will not be too trusting.

Is there another facet to being 'childlike'? The answer is 'yes'. There is another trait that kids have that they lose all too soon: an insatiable curiosity, coupled with great joy in learning something new, or finding the answer to a question that has been hanging fire for a while. Even in the days when I would not get involved with the world, I always was like that, and from that high school sophomore year onward, it consumed me.

I have to wonder, why do people lose the ability to wonder? At what point do they need to be 'cool'? I see that as quite unfortunate. These people are missing what could be a very full life. It is almost as if their epitaphs would read: 'Died at twenty-five; buried at seventy-five'.

2   Matthew 18:3.
3   Matthew 7:15.
4   I Corinthians 13:11.

Values that were Manifested During Military Service

Similar to the idea of being a 'loner' is the notion of not being a 'team player'. This explains many of the successes and failures that I have had in my life.

I served in the Army for about three and a half years, starting in October 1954. I spent one and a half years as an enlisted man and two years as an officer. I remember that, as an enlisted man, I decided I did not want to be a follower. After I became an officer, I realized that I was equally uncomfortable being a leader. I felt extremely vulnerable in either rôle.

Considering what I have written, in a later section, about being neither competitive nor ambitious, the most rewarding assignment that I had in the army was not as an officer, but the last one that I held as an enlisted man. I was fire-director and computer (FDC) for an 81mm mortar platoon. The significance of this bears some explanation.

Heavy, high-trajectory weapons, such as these, are usually placed toward the rear, where they cannot see the target area. There is a forward observer (FO) who can see the target, but is generally looking at it from a completely different direction than the one from which the guns face the target. Consequently, any changes ordered by the FO, in range and direction, for the purpose of adjusting fire on the target, will be irrelevant to the changes the guns have to make.

My job was to make the necessary transformations from the FO's corrections to those required by the guns, and to issue fire commands to the guns.

I was outranked in that platoon by the platoon leader (an officer), the platoon sergeant, the gun crew commanders, and even some members of the gun crews themselves. That did not bother me in the slightest because, in that organization, I possessed a unique skill, and everybody, from the platoon leader on down, depended on my expertise for that unit's effectiveness.

I was a one-man band in doing this, and was not a member of any of the gun crews. This dovetailed perfectly with my predilection for doing things in a solitary manner.

I suppose that, to many (if not most) people, there is a certain amount of ego-feeding satisfaction to be gained from being an officer. You get to wear glitter on your uniform that clearly identifies to all what you are, people stand at attention and call you 'Sir' when you talk to them, and you get to boss people around.

It did not take me long to realize that all of this added a whole new meaning to the word 'vainglory'. I was ultimately impressed by none of it, and it paled next to the job satisfaction that I got as FDC of that mortar platoon.

Interactions with Others

When the time came for me to be discharged, I decided that the thing I would like to do best was to be an expert at something, since I wanted to be neither a leader nor a follower. I would not have to supervise others in a personal sense. I would work for others, but, instead of simply being given orders by them, they would come to me for the advice that they had to have in order to accomplish their objectives.

It was for this reason that I went back to school to do graduate study in physics and mathematics. (A coinciding reason was that, by that time, I had totally despaired of ever making sense out of human nature or behavior.) It prepared me well for the sort of thing that I did best.

(Incidentally, long before I read the article, I remember saying to my doctor, 'I seem to be able to give another person some kind of love under the right conditions, but I do not seem to be able to accept it'. He nodded knowingly. I wonder if he suspected even then.)

For this reason, if I do connect with another person, it is because we have a compatibility, and not in order to fill some emotional need. (I often refer to the latter as 'feeding on someone emotionally'. This may seem harsh, but it is the way I see it.)

From the other person's point-of-view, there are one benefit and two drawbacks. The benefit is that the other person can know that my favor is freely given, with no possessiveness, and that this other person will be given all the space that he or she could possibly need. (Likewise, a cat can be affectionate, not because she has to or needs to, but because she wants to.)

The first drawback is that my attachment can be relatively easily alienated, since I do not cling to a relationship that I see as counter-productive in order to keep a void filled. The second is that the other person does not have the feeling of being 'needed'. I have been led to understand that this is supposed to be quite important to most people, who would otherwise feel insecure.

I imagine that, whatever the rewards might be, there can be a significant downside to 'needing' to be loved. It could drive one to give love to another person unwisely, in the hope that this love might be returned. I can only speculate on the pain that this could cause, should that love prove to be misplaced. This would be due to the fact that being able to feel the *agape* type of love gives one a vulnerability not shared by me or others like me.

This sort of thing goes back to my earliest childhood memories. I never really wanted to play with other kids, preferring, instead, activities that were solitary. These included reading, learning, art (about this more later), and, from the age of twelve onward, classical music.

One fallout from this is that, if other people could not give me emotional pleasure, neither could they cause me emotional pain. I have never in my life suffered because of anybody else's displeasure. (There is nothing anyone can say that would insult me or hurt my feelings. The best have tried and failed.) I can think of three examples.

It has been said that a prime candidate for someone who will rough up a child is the mother's boyfriend or second husband. The latter was the case with me, from the age of six until I was ten. My mother was recovering from tuberculosis and, as such, was feeling quite weak all the time. At this time, I was extremely hyperactive due to the neurological damage caused by being stricken with scarlet fever when I was a preschooler. At any number of times, when my stepfather came home, my mother lay in bed, exhausted.

He immediately, in each case, sized up the situation, and would punish me severely, both physically and verbally. The beatings hurt for a short while, but, strange to the ears of most people, the verbal abuse did not. The latter took an interesting form. He would tell me, in no uncertain terms, that not only was I excess baggage that came along with the deal when he married my mother, but also, if anything happened to her, he would hold me personally responsible.

It might seem that such things would be emotionally devastating to such a young child, but they rolled off me like the proverbial water off a duck's back. Looking back, I now realize that I have never had any emotions to devastate. Most people either repress memories of childhood traumas or are pained by them into adulthood. I remember them clearly, but with indifference.

(If I did have emotional capability, but repressed those emotions because they were too painful, then there is no way I could have avoided making someone like Woody Allen look like an individual who had it all together. Furthermore, it would burst the bonds of coincidence to have had such a repression of emotions be responsible for the abrupt and drastic change in my personality that took place during the year and a half of those onslaughts on my nervous system.)

The second instance took place in a classroom shortly after World War II started, when I was just shy of ten years old. The teacher was going through the roster of the entire class, pairing each child's name with his or her ethnic background. (In those days, it was called 'nationality'.) The familiar litany was sounded, reflecting the polyglot makeup of New York City at that time: Irish, Italian, Jewish, Polish, and so on.

When she called my name, she intoned, 'German'. A gasp went up from all the other pupils, and they turned toward me with horrified looks, as though I were dressed in the uniform of the *Hitler Jugend*[1] It did not seem to occur to the large group of Italian kids that their *Duce*[2] was allied with Hitler.

I was, for quite a while, treated as a pariah, and was subjected to epithets such as, 'You Nazi bastard'. However, being by myself had been, more or less, my natural state and the taunts left me totally unmoved, one way or the other.

As to the third item, in order to understand it, a discussion of my interaction with members of the opposite sex, during my adolescence and young adulthood, is in order.

When I hit adolescence, I was decidedly different from the image that teen-age girls of that time considered to be as attractive. Wavy hair was in; mine was straight. Big muscles were all the rage; I was, to be blunt, skinny. Being athletic and a good dancer were *de rigueur*; the effects of scarlet fever, mentioned above, left me without the necessary coordination or sense of timing to be either. A high premium was placed on being a 'snappy dresser'; I have always found fads in fashion to be grotesque. One was expected to like (or at least pretend to like) what the current vogue was in popular music; I was, as I still am, a totally unreconstructed classical music buff. In order to get along, one was expected not to excel in school too much; I not only took pride in my good grades, but enjoyed the company of adults because I could hold conversations on their level.

All of this, to put it mildly, added up to not being particularly sought after by girls my age. For a while, during my high-school freshman year, this bothered me. I then decided that I would rather do without, than either try to shoehorn myself into being someone that I wasn't, or to

1   Hitler Youth.
2   Mussolini's title; literally 'leader'.

subject myself to the indignity of being considered somebody's consolation prize. As a result, I did not date a girl until my high school senior prom and, looking back, I feel that I was pressured into doing that by some teachers who felt worried by my being so socially inert.

Due to this, I was never bothered by the myriad things females say to males in order to bruise their egos by calling their masculinity into question. (Sometimes I get the impression that they must stay up nights thinking up these things.) I remember them all doing a slow burn when I would shrug my shoulders at what they said. (One egregious example was, 'You make love in a very businesslike manner.')[3] In fact, this shoulder-shrugging is precisely the reaction I have always given to any insult or put-down I ever got from anybody.

How did I spend my teen years? I spent them going to operas, concerts, and museums. I frequented the libraries and read as much as I could. I also engaged in conversation with the few friends I did make (mostly adults) about art, music, science, literature, and philosophy. It could possibly be said that, in doing this, I neglected the development of necessary social skills.

I wonder if it would have done any good if I had tried to be a 'mixer'. As an Army officer, later on, I had to do a do-it-yourself crash course in off-duty socializing, but my greatest successes consisted in staying out of the way of other people. To this day, avoiding social *gaucherie* requires a constant conscious effort. But, isn't that one of the hallmarks of autism?

From what I have read, being such an odd man out, vis-à-vis the adolescent mainstream, has often been enough to make someone into either a gang member or a teen-age suicide. I used to practically dislocate my shoulder from patting myself on the back for having had the strength of character to refuse to 'give in to peer pressure' in order to avoid these two calamities, but now, of course, I realize that I was not making any hard choices at all. This is one of the ways that the discovery of my autism has helped keep up my quota of humility.

I guess that this is one reason that the only group of God's creatures that I have been able to relate to well is cats. One cannot have a good relationship with a cat if one gets upset about what can be perceived as rejection, or if one is unable to give love without worrying about getting it

---

3   These days, 'making love' is a euphemism for sexual copulation. At that time, that was specifically excluded when using this expression. I don't want anyone to get the mistaken impression that my life has been more interesting than it actually has been.

back. Furthermore, cats appear to exhibit many of the character traits of the HFA person.

Of course, one pitfall of being invulnerable to insults is an inadvertent insensitivity to the sensibilities of others. It is hard, when one cannot be hurt, to anticipate the possible hurts of others. On more than one occasion, I have been thankful that my foot size is only seven and a half. For this reason, avoiding hurting the feelings of others, like maintaining minimal social graces, is something I have always had to work at diligently.

How should I like people to be toward me in this regard? Don't be polite; be candid.

Art as an Early Outlet

The principal subject of the *New Yorker* article displayed the *savant* part of his autism through an early manifestation of talent in art. I showed such an aptitude myself in first grade. (For one example of this, from my early adolescence, which has survived all of my relocations, see the last page.)

I remember that I would draw things rather realistically in minute detail, much to the astonishment of my teacher. I balked at painting with the brushes that the school provided because they could not allow me to achieve the fine details that a pencil or pen could. This preference followed me all my life. This has caused me to prefer black-and-white to color, even in photography. Oddly, I am physically sensitive to small differences in color, but I am indifferent to it aesthetically.

They teach kids in school to paint the sky by using a wide band of blue across the top of the picture, leaving the rest of the paper blank as though the sky were stark white down to the horizon. I remember the teacher being amazed when I painted the blue all the way down to the horizon. She took me to the window and pointed out to me how light the sky was at the horizon. I pointed out to her that the change was gradual, not abrupt, and that the sky never did get to be completely white, not even at the horizon.

Later on, mostly in high school, as mentioned above, I took to other intellectual and aesthetic pursuits, as did the subject child in the article. This is why the premium on logic and rationality (together with minimalization of the emotions), of which I wrote above, has always come to me so easily; almost, in fact, naturally.

I might mention, at this point, that I went to one of New York's specialized high schools, where the student body, rather than being from some neighborhood, was drawn from the entire city, and where entrance was by competitive examination. Mine gave exhaustive concentrations in art and music, as well as the full normal academic curriculum.

I remember one incident, during my senior year in high school, that illustrates this. In a French class, we were reading a short story, written in the first person of the wife of a French naval officer. I was translating a passage in which she described her pain and sorrow at their separations during his frequent and lengthy sea exercises.

The teacher asked me if I understood why she felt that way. To me, logic dictated that, if she could not tolerate lengthy absences by her husband, then surely there were other advantageous marriages that she could have made other than to a Navy officer. I answered the teacher's question, 'No, why should she?' Both the teacher and the students groaned. Already I had gained a reputation. (The teacher, at one time, described me as 'l'homme au cœur de pierre'.)[1] In connection with this, one of my schoolmate friends called me a 'paradox on wheels'.

Earlier, I wrote about how I would not take part in the classroom work, but would absorb the material being taught. A few understanding teachers, realizing this, let me sit in the back of the class and draw pictures.

1   'The man with a heart of stone'.

Religion

How has my autism affected my religious beliefs?

Temple Grandin, in her autobiography[1] has written about the fact that, while she was raised an Episcopalian (a church with a structured organization and formal theology), her religious beliefs have evolved into those that are based on logic rather than faith and appear to stem, in an *ad hoc* manner, from addressing specific questions.

While my current beliefs do involve a structured church and formal theology, my own spiritual odyssey has come to the same destination (although I treat the existence of God in the more general context of a question of whether or not the universe had a beginning, which I feel is a scientific hypothesis, more in the domain of the physicist than the theologian), but its origin could not have been more different.

I am a practising Roman Catholic, but am an adult convert to that faith. It may even be a misnomer to call that odyssey 'spiritual' since its beginning was anything but that. My family were all atheists, and I was raised to be one. In early adolescence, I began to question all that. There were two reasons.

The first is the discovery I made at that time that, far from being, of their own essence, tolerant and open-minded, nonbelievers can be just as dogmatic, self-righteous, guilt-peddling, and judgmental as the most hard-shell religious fundamentalists.

The second involves the fact that, from the time that I became politically aware (at the age of twelve) I have had a social conscience. It occurred to me that this social conscience was resting on shifting sand unless it depended on objective truth and an ethical system that had a basis other than whose ox is being gored.

Atheism completely failed that last test. If a person's material interests ran counter to my perception of social and economic justice, on what basis could I possibly be expected to appeal to that person? This would also

---

1   Grandin, Temple (1995) *Thinking in Pictures.* New York: Doubleday.

apply to a person with no particular interests. Why should he or she be sympathetic to my idea of justice rather than the opposite?

In a typical manner, I decided to study the beliefs and teachings of a number of different religions. (When I get interested in something, I go into it total immersion.) By the time that I was an undergraduate in college, I had determined that Catholicism had the ideal mix: orthodox and rational in its theology, but liberal and progressive in its teachings on social and economic matters.

All of this amounts to metaphysical and ethical systems[2] that I had believed for some time, and had found, as I said, to be unsupported by an atheistic philosophy. A major part of the Church's ethical system, that appealed to me, was its position on conflict resolution, which I believe to be the only one that would give a foundation for real peace.

There is one point of view that every conflict contains a solution that will fulfill the expectations of all parties involved. This would state that there should really be no cause for the conflict in the first place (the 'give peace a chance' outlook). This was Hegel's position,[3] and I find it, at best, quite naïve.

Using an analogy in physics, peace is a state that is essentially unstable. To upset it, it only takes one party that feels aggrieved. The other parties will not seek to restore it if they also feel themselves basically unhappy with the situation.

Marx was able to point out that there exist conflicts in which the parties' interests are mutually exclusive. One can only benefit at the expense of the others. In his view, there are 'our' interests (the good guys) and 'their' interests (the bad guys). It would be unrealistic even to attempt compromise, since each side would wait for an opportunity to reclaim their lost interests. Anything else goes totally against human nature. Thus, to protect 'our' interests, 'they' must be totally vanquished.[4] Even when there is talk of 'compromise', it is in the spirit of: 'To show what good guys we are, let's give something to the bad guys, so they'll go away.'

This attitude, it always seemed to me, cannot help but set the stage for the next outbreak. The only way I could see around it was given, in 1891,

---

2   These would give a framework in which one could see the universe, one's place in it, and the interaction with others.

3   From the thesis and antithesis, we get the synthesis.

4   Given this, it is not inconceivable that the adversary principle, on which the American judicial system rests, could be said to derive from Marxist ethics.

by Pope Leo XIII.[5] His ideas were ratified by the Second Vatican Council.

This approach takes, as its basis, the notion that, in a conflict, each party has legitimate interests. These must be recognized, and accepted as such, by the other parties. If the negotiations can be brought to a point at which each party believes its interests to have been optimized, the resulting agreement would be stable, because, if one party tried to upset the agreement, the others would have an incentive to bring that party back into line. Such a point could be called 'justice'.[6]

I also could not help but notice that, in the Hebrew Scriptures, instead of communicating directly with people in some manner, God sent prophets to them to let His will be known. This is a mechanism that could be called: working for people through people. That mechanism became evident to me in my study of each of the Catholic Church's sacraments.

There is yet another characteristic of the sacraments that bears heavily on what I wrote earlier about my desire for certainty in things (not unrelated to my predilection for mathematics). In the gospels, during His earthly ministry, Jesus made a number of promises to people. In each of the sacraments, there is the absolute certainty of those promises being fulfilled.

There are many people who claim that adopting a religion 'changed their lives'. The most famous case of an enormous change is that of John Newton, who wrote *Amazing Grace*. As a result of his conversion, he went from being the captain of a slave-transporting ship to one of Europe's leading crusaders against slavery.

The character of my own conversion was quite different. My ideas about the responsibilities, as members of society, that people have for themselves and to each other, remained essentially unchanged. I was not a bad person prior to becoming a Catholic, nor did I become materially better afterward. I felt that my beliefs now had a rock-solid basis.

It must be pointed out explicitly that none of this has any emotional underpinnings, but is totally intellectual in its nature. It has always been that way with me. When a woman, who was a classmate of mine in high school, wrote a letter of recommendation for me, she said that my ideas and attitudes were 'based on intellectual determinants'.

---

5   In his encyclical *Rerum Novarum*, which set the Church's view on social and economic issues. While addressing the conditions of labor, he challenged Marx's idea of the inevitability of class warfare.

6   This would be rationale behind those bumper stickers that read: 'If you want peace, work for justice'.

I have not, as so many people do, gotten any solace or comfort from my religion, nor have I ever sought any. I have been told, from many quarters, that, even with intellectual conviction, a religion is useless without a 'gift of the Spirit', and that, if this gift is received, no such conviction is necessary.

I just cannot relate to that; I have never felt such a 'gift'. To me, as far as adherence to a religion (or any other type of ideology) is concerned, intellectual conviction is a condition that mathematicians call 'both necessary and sufficient'. My religious faith, I guess I could say, is not a gift from God, as so many people say; it is a gift I gave to myself.

In line with this, I have never felt the emotional exhilaration that people must feel when they have a 'religious experience'. This is true even when I receive the sacraments. The only thing that has deeply moved me is the *reasonableness* of it all.

The Doctrine of the Trinity is called a 'mystery'. To me, when one considers the explanation of the Doctrine of Processions,[7] then the Trinity falls out from that by simple use of mathematical logic. The kinds of things that are mysteries to me are the Wave-Particle Duality,[8] and, of course, human nature and behavior. The first I hope will be explained during my lifetime; I totally despair of ever understanding the second.

I realize that all of this might cause me to run afoul of what St Paul said about the *agape* kind of love in I Corinthians 13:2.[9] This is to say that, without it, knowledge and conviction just do not amount to anything. But, as I said above, that happens to be the way I am.

7   The Holy Spirit as the bond of love between the Father and the Son.
8   On the sub-atomic level, waves, which are continuous, and particles, which are discrete, each exhibit the properties of the other.
9   'If I have knowledge to understand all mysteries and faith enough to move mountains, but do not have love, I have nothing.'

Disclaimers about Religion

In the previous chapter, I described my conversion to Catholicism, and my rationale for doing so. Often, when I mention this to someone, I discover that the person with whom I am talking has been raised as a Catholic but, for a number reasons, has left the Church.

(I discovered a way to defuse this situation. I say that St Peter, looking at our conversation, must be saying to himself: 'Well, you win some and you lose some.')

Taking the view that someone who disagrees with me may have good reasons for doing so, I usually ask why they left. Their answers often turn out to be instructive.

My conversion took place in the bad old days before Vatican II. Many of those people told me that they left the Church because of painful childhood memories of that era, attributing many of their psychological problems to their youthful Catholic upbringing. They asked me how I could have voluntarily joined such an institution. Implicit in this is a questioning of my credibility on other things.

Over and over, I hear the stories of martinet priests and nuns, who lay on major guilt by portraying God as someone who plays 'gotcha', who tell you that your non-Catholic friends are going to hell, and that the worst sins are missing mass and eating meat on Friday, etc., etc. In addition, there were all those superstitious ideas and practices that, in many cases, bordered on idolatry.

All of these things were no more palatable to me than they were to those people who left the Church. One of the reasons it took so long for me to make the commitment to become a Catholic, is that I had to ask myself, in so many instances, 'Will I have to believe that?' and 'Will I have to do that?' I was able to make the decision when I had given myself a sufficient number of 'No' answers to those questions.

One red-flag item is that of pedophile priests. Time after time, I hear this blamed on the Church's requirement that its clergy be celibate. I believe that celibacy is a phony issue. There are instances galore of pedophilia and other sexual misconduct by clergy of other faiths and lay people, all of whom could have healthy sexual outlets if they so chose.

Priests, who do these things, ill-use those who have totally put their trust in them. They are not alone. They have nothing on many in the mental health industry. In this latter case, even those who do not do that, routinely cover up for those who do. (Is there any profession or trade in which that does not happen these days?)

It is not only boys who are at risk. A few years back, an archbishop in the southwestern United States had to resign when it was revealed that he had, years before as a priest, seduced a number of Catholic high school girls.

There are, and have been, bad priests, bad bishops, even bad popes. Should we judge the Church, and Catholicism, by them? Consider democracy. Phenomena like Huey Long and Joe McCarthy could only have happened in a democracy. Hitler came to power in an open, fair, and free election. Should we judge democracy by them?

As a case in point, one of the things I had to face up to was the first bishop I had. (It was before Vatican II, so the reforms had not yet started to take effect.) In his archdiocese, workers were so poorly paid that they had to get supplementary welfare in order for their families to survive. When the grave diggers in the archdiocesan cemeteries, as a last resort, formed a union and struck for higher wages, he brought in seminary students to be used as scabs.

An important distinction has to be made. Those things that attracted me to the Church were its 'teachings', which is the essence of the Church. The day-to-day visible practices are the institutional church, composed of fallible human beings.

What this amounted to was to embrace the Catholic faith and participate in its sacramental life, while keeping the institutional church at arm's length. That is part of the broader ability I seem to have, in order to focus on the good essence of something, to look beyond the bad peripherals and, if need be, tune those out.

When I speak of a dichotomy between the Church's teachings[1] and the institutional church, the germ of this was brought to me decades ago, when

[1] This is taken to mean those things that have been doctrinally defined, either by ecumenical councils, or by popes who have explicitly invoked infallibility. (This has been done only twice: in 1854, for The Immaculate Conception, and in 1950, for The Assumption.) All others are the Church's official position, but are not binding on Catholics.

I was studying those teachings, trying to find out if they did indeed mirror my own metaphysics and ethics. As I have mentioned, I could not possibly have taken that step without this.

Most priests that I dealt with were, at best, disturbed by my inquisitiveness, which was geared toward getting below the surface of the usual course of study. I wanted to dispel my doubts by going into the nuances and subtleties of the subject matter, and find out if I really agreed with it.

Having mostly dealt with people who had an 'experience', and would accept things without question, these priests tended to lose patience with someone who wanted intellectual conviction, and who could not accept anything less. I had abandoned a philosophy that, on intellectual grounds, I had found wanting, and did not want to repeat that experience by accepting anything uncritically.

A college friend of mine referred me to a priest friend of his, who was also a Benedictine monk. That priest took all the time I needed to discuss my doubts. He was able to explain the teachings to my satisfaction, but then, from time to time, I would bring up to him those many Church practices that irritated me as well as others. (These were those things for which the institutional church would be responsible.) His answer was, invariably, along the lines of: 'In light of what you seem to have found in the Church, do you really want to let that bother you?'

All of this may ring somewhat hollow to people who can see only that they left a church that made them miserable and that I voluntarily chose that church. They must feel that, even if the church today is different, I chose the church that caused them to want to leave.

The changes that have taken place since Vatican II were changes that I advocated before anybody even considered a Vatican II. I consider it a privilege to have seen it all happen.[2] There are many in the Church who opposed that Council's reforms. They would like nothing better than to see people who support those reforms leave. They could then point to us and say that the reformers are unfaithful Catholics. If nothing else, I do not want to give them that satisfaction.

It took ten years before I saw a manifestation of the reasons that I joined. It was in the early 1960s, and I went to mass in a church located in suburban Long Island, NY. There was an important issue at that time so, on

---

2   There are two ways you know that you are getting old. One is when the rest of the world leaves you behind. The other is when the rest of the world catches up with you.

this Sunday, the pastor gave the sermon at all masses (it is usually given by the celebrant).

He said that some Black families were buying homes in the area, and told the parishioners that these people should be welcomed, and that panic selling should be avoided. What struck me particularly was his opening choice of words: 'As you know, the newspapers have reported that Negro families are moving into our neighborhood, and I want to take this opportunity to remind you of your moral obligations as Catholics.'

Recently, a young non-Catholic woman and I were discussing capital punishment. She was for it; I am against it. We argued back and forth, neither of us making a dent in the other's position. She finally decided that we should agree to disagree. It was the words she chose to do this that I find memorable: 'Ed, you're a Catholic, so I expect you to be against the death penalty.'

A Perhaps Dangerous Characteristic

There is yet another symptom of autism to which I can relate. When one sees a group of autistic children, there will be some that will be wearing headgear that look like football helmets. This is because it is feared that they will hurt themselves by banging their heads against walls. What is happening is that, when their rage becomes uncontrollable (for whatever reason), they turn that rage first against inanimate objects, and then, should their anger not yet be spent, against themselves.

About a year before my first nervous breakdown, at the peak of a shouting match with my family, I slashed my forearm with my straightedge razor. At the time, I and everyone else took it as a suicide attempt. Now that I look back on it, I did *not* want to die. When my anger boiled over, I turned it against myself.

(Before my wife and I married, she had told me that my mother had told her that, when I was young, whenever I got angry I would hurt myself before I would hurt anyone else.)

In light of this, it might perhaps be advisable for an autistic person's dwelling (assuming he can function as such) to be for him alone. Anyone who shares that dwelling must be willing to give him all the space that he needs. But, isn't that what cat lovers do for their feline companions?

The Upshot of this Self-Discovery

People whom I know to care about me have expressed concern about the effect that this realization of my autism has had on me. In particular, they worry that I may have discovered that there is something 'wrong' with me. Very much to the contrary! It was quite liberating. It was that schizophrenia diagnosis that had made me feel almost subhuman. When this sort of thing is told to you authoritatively, you cannot help but wonder what ever happened to the person who, in your heart of hearts, you know you are, and where that imposter came from who is now occupying your soul.

Since that initial discovery, I have learned a great deal about autism, both on my own and in consultation with experts. Each new thing that I found out gave me a deeper insight into what and who I am, and why I do the things I do in the ways that I do them. Far from being disturbed by these insights, this self-knowledge has enabled me to accept myself to a degree that I never have before. The only way that I can express this is that I may perhaps be called unconventional, even perhaps eccentric, but certainly no oddball.

One interesting thing that I read is that an autistic person will *not* consciously be a manipulator of other people. (He or she may try to do that, but will not be any good at it.) I wondered why that might be so, and concluded that it was related to the emotional deficit. In order to manipulate another, it is necessary to get inside that person's emotions. This can only be done if you can connect them with your own emotions, which, of course presupposes having emotions of your own. Also, it requires a predisposition to control other people. Autistic people very much want to control, but *only* what they consider their space, preferring people to be there by invitation only.

(Unless they feel threatened, they issue that invitation on a very regular basis. In my own case, everybody whom I have not explicitly *dis*invited has a standing invitation.)

I have written about autistic people being protective of their 'space', as though it were some sort of psychological realm in which they might wish to remain secluded, inviting someone else in only when it is felt to be safe to do so. There is also, in some cases, a physical space involved.

That teacher of autistic children invited me to observe her class. I saw there, in that class, a rather extreme case of that. When the class went outside for recess, there was one boy who was shooting baskets with one of the other teachers. When I tried to walk up to the teacher to talk to her, the boy interrupted his play and pushed me off the court with all of the strength he could summon. When this happened a couple of times more, I contented myself with shouting at the teacher from the sidelines.

I am in no way as intense about my space as that boy was, but I do understand his feelings perfectly.

The bright side of this is that an autistic person will, in all likelihood, never be a stalker or an abuser. Also, since salesmanship (or any other form of persuasion) involves a certain amount of manipulation, the downside is that we would be very bad at that. I have always known that, unless I could point out to him the logic of his predicament, I could never sell a life raft to a drowning sailor. Now I know why.

A companion trait to not being a manipulator is that an autistic person, conversely, cannot be manipulated, and for much the same reason; he does not have emotions for another person to get into. Two characteristics of mine that possibly relate to this are that I am totally noncompetitive and I am not in the least ambition-driven.

As to not being competitive, the only card game I ever play is solitaire (the only game absolutely *requiring* honesty). I hate to play games in which scores are kept. The only condition under which I will play something like tennis is if all we do is hit the ball back and forth. Perhaps the root of this is that I do not measure myself against others, but only my own internal standards.

This even applies to endeavors in which I know that I excel. I like games like *Trivial Pursuit* and *Jeopardy* because they enable me to test my knowledge against myself. I get fidgety when the other players keep score, even though I am usually ahead.

There was an incident that illustrates this. I used to belong to a club whose members would sometimes watch *Jeopardy* in the evening. I would give each answer that I knew before the contestant on the show did so. I never kept score as to how much I would have won, but one of the other members told me that, if I could be chosen as a contestant, he would pay my expenses there and back in return for ten percent of my winnings.

I would not have taken him up on it. As a contestant, I would have had to keep score and that would have totally ruined my enjoyment.

To show the extent to which I am not driven to win, when I play solitaire, I modify the rules to make it more difficult to win. I want winning to be a banner occasion, not an everyday occurrence. That way, I *really* enjoy it.

I am not ambitious because I do not seek to hold a particular rank in an organization; to me those are empty honors. Using those internal standards mentioned above, I want to do the work that is up to my level of capability, and which I feel is essential to the mission of the organization.

Being noncompetitive and non-ambitious has a further consequence. Those who are competitive and ambitious put a high premium on 'coming out on top'. They seek out situations in which they can do this, if such situations do not occur in the normal course of events. As such, they become confronters, and actually relish confrontations.

But, this requires an emotional interaction with the person being confronted. The implication is that an autistic person will not be a confronter, but, rather, a conciliator. One drawback to this is that a confronter sees any attempt at conciliation as a sign of weakness, and usually moves to exploit it. To my detriment, this has happened to me a number of times in my life.

I have always found competition, confrontation, and other such 'power games' to be extremely distasteful, engaging in them only under the most extreme necessity. When one considers that, by my nature, I am limited in the ways in which I am able to interact with other people, one should imagine how it must be, for me, to have to interact under such unpleasant circumstances. The way that I function may be incomprehensible to most people, but it never ceases to mystify me that other people do these things for enjoyment.

Is a Future Close
Relationship Possible?

One important point that I should like to make is: it stands to reason that, when a person with deep emotional needs tries to connect with someone incapable of having such needs (and who may even consider this an intrusion), then the emotional person will be hurt, unless he or she has understanding and compassion that approaches the extraordinary (again, in the literal sense of that word: from the Latin for 'outside' the ordinary). Because of this, the non-emotional person must perhaps confine himself to 'arms-length' relationships, and must take the initiative to keep it that way if it looks like it is going to get any closer than that. There are occasions, in everyone's life, when the greatest gift of love one can give to another is one's absence. In my case, that occasion could very well be my entire life-span.

This is as good a place as any to address the question: is it possible for a NT ('neurologically-typical') woman to have a successful marriage with somebody with AS or HFA? This is quite analogous to the problems faced by a woman contemplating marriage to a blind man. I refer to my previous remark about each missing an important faculty possessed by most people. This is a subject that I can approach with some authority, because I can now look back at almost an entire lifetime of attempts at relationships that, in one way or another, failed.

I have limited this to those two types of autism because, if there is no communication capability, then it is an open question as to whether or not *any* kind of parity relationship is even possible. Even if he has no emotions to express, he *must* be able to express his thoughts.

(In addition, I have limited myself to an examination of a woman with full faculties and either a blind or an autistic man. I am not totally insensitive to the problems faced by women with these missing faculties, but I have no means whatsoever of identifying with them.)

Before beginning, the question must be raised as to why we should even be considering this issue. After all, the autistic man cannot emotionally connect with her so, as they say, 'What's in it for her?' Here is where we resurrect a previous observation about an autistic man developing his intellectual and aesthetic capabilities as compensation for his emotional deficit.

If the woman herself is intellectually and aesthetically inclined (and is capable of treating such things separately from personal emotions) she could be able to share these things in a way that she could not with an NT man, and this could form a very tight bond between them. Shakespeare, in a way, recognized this when he began his 116th sonnet with the words: 'Let me not to the marriage of true minds admit impediments'.

As to the aesthetic in particular, would a woman mind it very much if, instead of merely being something that causes his testosterone to rumble, he were to look at her the same way that he would look at a Rubens painting, a Bernini sculpture, or a Gothic cathedral?

Consider what would happen at the outset of a relationship. The blind man might run his fingers over the woman's face and say, 'God, but you are so beautiful'. The response of most women, in thought if not in speech, would be, 'How would you know? You can't even see me'. By the same token, a woman might dismiss an autistic man's expressions of the *philos* type of love as shallow and meaningless, because they are not accompanied by the 'warmth' that accompanies *agape*.

In both cases, the woman has to be aware that the man has developed his other faculties to compensate for the one that is missing. The blind man's fingers can 'feel' her beauty as much as the sighted man's eyes. The autistic man's *philos* should not be dismissed as *ersatz* love. He can respond to the woman with total commitment, if not with warmth. It must also be remembered that, with his heightened aesthetic sensibility, he might very well view her, if not merely as a sex object, as a work of art of nature.

If she does decide to marry the man with the missing faculty, she must be aware that there will have to be some lifestyle changes. These changes are generally in the category of being constantly conscious of things that she normally took for granted to the point of mindlessness. She cannot assume anything, and must be aware of what these changes are and accept them without any equivocation or reservations, or any feelings that she has for him will start to wear thin before long.

Some of these changes involve possible physical dangers. How often do sighted people put something down in the middle of the floor when they are distracted by something else? The blind man has had to make sure that all possible pathways in his home are kept clear. He might trip and hurt himself should something be there of which he is not aware.

By the same token, she would have to be aware that her autistic husband does not possess the same fear of physical danger and sensitivity to pain that she does. Often, when I bake, I am quite cavalier about taking things in and out of hot ovens. When I run things down the garbage disposer and something gets stuck in the opening, I often, without thinking, poke it down with my fingers. Her antenna for danger just might make life a bit less risky for him, if she does not get sick and tired of having to watch out for all that.

In connection with that, for almost thirty years, I have shaved with a straightedge razor. I started on the advice of a barber, who suggested it when I complained about constantly cutting myself with 'safety' razors. Once he showed me how to use it, I had no trepidation and was not bothered by the nicks I got in my earliest attempts. I still do it as a snob thing since it does require a unique skill.

Both the blind and autistic man have a great need for routine that should only be disturbed for good reason. The autistic man might look at any unanticipated attempt at changing a routine as an intrusion into his space, and might instinctively become self-protective, at least initially. His wife must take care not to spring surprises on him, even pleasant ones.

However, the blind man needs a routine of sorts also. Sighted people leave things every which where, and glance around when they want to find them. The blind have to keep everything in specific places so that they may know where to go to feel for them. The sighted wife must be consciously careful not to leave things in places where they are not normally found. In addition, she should be careful in having a conversation with someone whose voice he does not recognize unless the other person is identified and he is included in the conversation.

There must be very few women with egos large enough to think that their femininity is so strong as to be able to restore sight to a blind man. Yet, inadvertent though it may be, many a woman might feel that the strength of her *agape* type of love will awaken it in an autistic man by somehow 'curing' his emotional deficit. Without some breakthrough in neurology, this simply cannot happen. She must appreciate the fact that his *philos* might possibly be as strong as, or stronger, than the *agape* of other men.

We must also consider what would happen if she wants to share with her husband what she considers to be a wonderful feeling, and does so in an instinctive manner, in ways in which he cannot respond.

The blind man's sighted wife might see an inspiring vista and blurt out, 'Look at that! Isn't it beautiful?' She will need to be able to find the spoken words to describe what she sees, cognizant of the fact that he has trained himself to respond to that sort of thing.

The autistic man's wife might look at him and, wanting to express her love for him, might want to rush over and hug and kiss him. She must be aware that autistic people, to some degree, have an aversion to being touched by other people[1] (cats are so like that). (Ironically, those who have the worst aversion seem to have no difficulty at all with physical contact with non-human animals.) She will have to find out the extent of that in him *before* they marry. If it is mild, she can approach him slowly, from where he can see her, and caress him gently. If his aversion to touch is strong, she can express her feelings for him verbally, making advantageous use of his strong aesthetic sensitivity.

Perhaps the most important question of all, to be asked of herself by a woman contemplating marriage to a man who is either blind or autistic, is this: how much does it count, in her life and for her feeling of personal fulfillment, to have children of her own? If the answer is 'a great deal', then she should seriously reconsider making such a marriage for herself.

The problems with the autistic husband are rather subtle. First, even though he might be able physically to see a dangerous situation, he very likely will not recognize it as such, which could leave the child exposed in a way similar to that of a blind father. There is a mitigating factor here in my case. Even though I am clueless about personal danger, I have found myself sensitive to danger to others.

Secondly, even if he is high functioning, and is especially sensitive to the beauty of a child, he will have great difficulty in communicating with that child on his or her own level.

I must bring to mind, at this point, the fact that, from early childhood, I preferred the company of adults to that of other children, and, as I grew older, I felt extreme difficulty knowing what to say to a child, unless he or she was precociously intelligent, even though I could spend hours looking at one who was beautiful.

Then there is an additional problem which I know of only from having been told: that the emotional development of a child is heavily dependent on the emotional rapport he or she has with his or her parents. This is said to involve a great deal of physical contact or, if you will, 'touching'.

1   This is a phenomenon called 'sensory overload', which is a sensation that is experienced by many NT when someone scratches a blackboard. It appears to be common, in varying degrees, in the autistic. Some are sensitive that way to certain colors, some to certain sounds, and others to certain touches.

Not having had any emotions to share since birth or early childhood, the man cannot supply this. His wife will have to do it all and, being aware of her husband's deficit, will have the double duty of seeing that the children do not take their father to task because he does not give what he does not have.

There are a number of other adjustments a woman must make for an autistic husband that do not relate to the situation of the blind man.

The first is that each must be quite explicit in expressing feelings, desires, and needs. Nuances and intuition are not to be used. The autistic man cannot; his wife should not. Ironically, it is much easier for the man to open up to his wife because he does not fear any rejection that might occur should he appear vulnerable. He cannot feel the pain of his wife, nor of any other person for that matter, but he *can* understand that she is troubled if it is explained to him.

There is a story that graphically illustrates what she must *not* do in this situation. A man's wife sits weeping. He asks her, 'What's wrong?' She says, 'You should know'. He then says, 'If I knew, I wouldn't have to ask'. To this, she replies, 'You shouldn't have to ask'. The autistic man has neither the antenna nor the receiver for unspoken emotional signals, let alone a decoder. She must let him know explicitly that something is bothering her, and what it is, giving specifics.

The one thing that can be required of him is to ask, 'What can I do to help you?' If she answers, giving specifics, she will find him a helpmate in every sense of that word. Otherwise, he will take her at her word that nothing is wrong and, believing that she only wants to be alone (a feeling to which he is no stranger), he will walk away from her, giving her the impression that he is cold and heartless.

The NT can play these games in a relatively harmless manner because they possess the antennae, receivers, and decoders that are necessary. For the autistic man and his wife, it could cause the relationship 'chemistry' eventually to turn sour.

To think of it, this is advice that is not too bad for couples where there is *no* autism involved. Most people might be afraid to be that open with one another because it would expose an emotional vulnerability that they are afraid will be exploited. I can afford to be that open because nature has shielded me from that kind of vulnerability.

She must take into account the fact that he is neither competitive nor ambition-driven. This might be quite difficult if she *is* those things herself, since she will always be measuring herself against what others have accomplished. The temptation, that so many competitive and ambitious people have, to feel contemptuous of those who are not, can be overwhelming. If she, no matter how much she might admire other qualities, cannot totally accept this characteristic in her husband, then it is a marriage that is doomed from the beginning.

She must be constantly aware that he cannot be a manipulator nor can he be manipulated. Manipulation implies a conscious effort on the part of the one doing this to influence the behavior of another. He is incapable of that, so she must not interpret any recalcitrance on his part as an attempt at manipulation. The only way to appeal to him is to be completely above board because he values rationality so much.

If the autistic partner is also obsessive-compulsive (at least in my use of the term), a possible accommodation is a clear-cut division of labor with regard to the household tasks. These tasks must be broken down so that each can do his or her own job in his or her own way.

She must be willing and able to totally accept all of these things. Yet, the worst thing that she must be willing to understand and accept is that, should she die, he will miss her very much, but will not suffer the pain of grief.

It must be reiterated here that this all pertains to things that a woman, married to either a sighted or an NT man, can take for granted in her daily life but, in these cases, must maintain constant awareness.

There is a way that an encapsulation of this can be expressed. A sighted woman lives in a world of light. Her blind husband lives in a world of darkness, bereft of light. An NT woman lives in a world that consists of both her mind and her heart. The world of her autistic husband consists only of his mind. Neither husband has chosen his world, but may have been able to more than compensate for his deficits.

The above demonstrates that finding a suitable and compatible mate for a man with either missing faculty is a tall order, but it is not impossible. The old bromide, 'There has to be someone out there for you,' is a cheap shot. There does not have to be, and there very well may not be.

We cannot, on the other hand, assume the opposite extreme: that there *cannot* be. I have heard that the only successful union that an autistic man can make is with an autistic woman. But this is the same as saying that a blind man should marry only a blind woman.

In this case, the two autistic people would probably both be loners, and should not live in close quarters unless they passionately share common interests. Those quarters should be sufficiently large to give plenty of space to each.

In a union between an autistic and an NT person, such as I have described, each member of the couple will certainly be able to relate easily to the other. In the case of each missing faculty, though, a person possessing that faculty *has* to be always aware of the other's limitations and strengths and be greatly appreciative of the latter.

This appreciativeness must be sufficient to enable any problems arising from that missing faculty to pale to insignificance (to employ a phrase used by a famous general). If, on the other hand, it is extremely important for her to be able to say either, 'I love the way he looks at me,' or 'the flow of warmth between us feels so good,' then there is hardly any hope at all.

What can the person with the missing faculty do? Most recovery programs place great emphasis on avoiding wishful thinking and connecting with realty, by distinguishing between those things that one can control and those that one cannot control, and dealing with each in its own appropriately effective manner. One is admonished to let go of the latter and to do what one must to effect the former. Any existence of 'someone out there' is one of those things that he cannot control. What he *can* control is allowing some room inside himself for her should she show up.

A good summary of such a policy would be: The door should not be locked shut, but neither should it be left standing open. Also, there should not be a 'Keep Out' sign on the door, but there should be one that says 'Please Knock Before Entering'.

This, of course, is something that can occur, if not only in the best of all possible worlds, then only under extremely limited circumstances. My own marriage had to be put out of its misery because we were not up to the Herculean task of making these adjustments. Ironically, because my discovery of my autism is so recent, neither of us was even aware that these adjustments needed to be made.

(For the record, she has no outrageously bad traits that are not shared abundantly by the rest of humanity. She very likely would have made a fantastic lifelong companion for a man who could have provided for her the essential missing ingredient that I never could.)

While making and maintaining such a union successfully may be theoretically possible, it will have to be for someone much more adventuresome than I am. There are two things that must be remembered: that, compared with the NT, I am at a considerable disadvantage at evaluating the sincerity of others' intentions, and that I would not so much as risk a dollar on a raffle ticket. As to the latter consideration, I would be wagering the rest of my life.

Given the size of the stakes involved and the astronomical odds against that union's success, while I plan to continue the rewarding friendships that I have made based on mutual interests (and even make new ones), my personal private life will, by comparison, make the Mount Athos Monastery[2] look like a Roman orgy.

2   A Greek Orthodox monastery, where the rule of life is ultra-ascetic.

Waxing Philosophical about 'Love' Among the Non-Autistic

The previous chapter dealt with the question of how an autistic man and an NT woman might be able to interact. I will now try to show how the world looks to me, in light of the way NT men and women appear to interact with each other.

From reports in the media, and even my personal observations, women appear to fall deeply in love (in the *agape* sense), and remain in love with and loyal to, alcoholics, drug addicts, bisexuals (who don't bother to inform them of that), career criminals, rapists, serial killers, men who physically abuse them, and even men who beat and kill their children.

On the other hand, looking back on my entire life, I, who am none of those things, have never had a woman fall in love with the *real* me. There were those who said they were attracted, but they all turned out eventually to have a (mostly secret) laundry list of changes they proposed to make in me, thus wanting to turn me into somebody else other than the real me. I must now restate the fact that this causes me no pain. I am simply standing in awe of the total absence of logic in all of this.

Had I known about my autism during those years, I certainly would have been candid about it with the women that I knew. Perhaps one or more of them just might have decided that she could and would be more than willing to make the required adjustments.

This, of course, did not happen, and, at this time, I can only speculate as to whether each woman that I knew did not somehow sense that there was a nutrient missing in the recipe and that, while I might have been good for an occasional repast (or even perhaps, for some of them, a feast), a steady diet of me would have, over time, resulted in emotional malnutrition for her.

The extent to which that nutrient is considered essential by NT women can be confirmed by that catalogue of horrors that they often seem to willingly endure in order to have it. Conceivably, one consolation that I can get out of all of this is that I might be able to take the fact that women *have not* seen fit to fall in love with the real me, and wear it like a badge of honor.

At this point, it might seem that I am waxing more cynical than philosophical. Cynicism is the inevitable result of losing one's illusions. If, together with the illusions, one also loses one's ideals, then the cynicism can be quite bitter. If, on the other hand, one manages to retain the ideals, a healthy cynicism results, that enables one to be more realistic about attaining those ideals.

I have observed a view of love, seemingly not only acceptable but rampant among humanity, that the Greeks seem never to have heard of. They probably would have had to coin a fourth word for it. I shall illustrate via three examples, the first two of which are hypothetical.

First, a man, seemingly unwilling or unable to take 'no' for an answer from a woman, resorts to what is called 'stalking'. She complains to the police and he is arrested. At the station house, he is confronted by his misdeeds: constantly telephoning her, ostentatiously loitering in front of her residence, banging on her front door demanding entry, and so on.

He is told that he is driving the poor woman to distraction, and that he must cease and desist, and is asked why he is doing these things. What he does *not* say is that he hates her with a passion and wants to make her life as miserable as possible. What he *does* say is that he loves her dearly, that she is obviously unaware of that, and that his persistence cannot help but win her over so that they might live happily together forever after.

A second example is that of a mistress who murders her lover's wife. When caught red-handed, she tells her lover, 'I did it for us, so that we could fully realize our love'. Furthermore, while shocked onlookers might deplore what she has done, she still garners a certain amount of sympathy because, 'She did it for love'.

The third case involves an incident in which a young man and woman (who were service academy cadets when arrested), when still in high school, brutally beat and murdered a sixteen-year-old girl. At that time, the young man and the young woman were an item. The woman came to believe that the man had sex with the future victim. She was livid, but later the two got together and made up. Absolutely OK about that. But then, according to the news article, the two murdered the sixteen-year-old 'as a way of reaffirming their love for each other'.

No matter which way I held the newspaper, that last sentence still read the same way. I would like to point out that the girl involved was brought to justice after she confided the murder to a roommate at the academy, and the roommate reported her. It is very reassuring that there are still places where refusal to 'not get involved' and 'look the other way' is alive and well.[1]

I must now couple these examples with an observation that I have made earlier in other contexts. It is that people tend to measure the sincerity and intensity of another person's love by the extent that he or she is willing to suffer.

Consider the phrases one hears all the time. 'Dying for love?' I should think that love would be something that would make one want to live. 'Lovesick?' I should think that love would be something that would make one healthier.

One other item about 'love' among the NT touches on an extremely controversial topic. Heterosexuals and homosexuals are at odds with each other (even when they try to do so in a civil manner) over questions such as whom you can love, whom you should love, and so on. They have in common what I believe to be a fallacious assumption that eclipses their differences: that 'whom you love' is identical to 'whom you want to have sex with'. Without that assumption, their differences evaporate.

I should like to refer to two of the three Greek words for 'love', *agape* and *eros*. Those words are *not* synonymous; they represent different ideas. I believe that there is a possibility of love without sex. According to modern theologians, that type of bond existed between Jesus and Mary Magdalen. It was true about Mother Teresa and others like her.

Yet, most people cannot seem to separate the one from the other. (They do not even consider *philos*.) When they refuse to consider a close relationship that will not lead to sex, they deprive themselves of many rewarding friendships. I was struck by a remark attributed to a woman who is a lesbian activist: 'The only queer people are those who don't love anybody'. She was talking about me and others like me.

There is much that is made of sexual compatibility. The bookshelves are lined with offerings on that topic. People seem to want to find that out even before they know the other's taste in coffee. Those books invariably concentrate on technique, with perhaps a genuflection or two toward things like kindness, generosity, or commonality of interests and values.

This is not to say that physical compatibility is a trivial consideration, but if a couple starts off with trying this out, I can see a problem. If it is good, the partner's bad traits are ignored; if it is less than good, the partner's good traits are overlooked.

---

1   The Code of Honor at the United States service academies reads: 'A cadet will not lie, cheat, or steal, nor tolerate those who do'.

I should like to offer my own modest idea of a test for sexual compatibility. There are a number of medical conditions, for men and women both, in which sexual functioning becomes impossible, or (worse yet) very painful. The test is in the form of a question one must ask himself or herself: should that happen to one's partner, would the bond between them break or even fray. If an honest answer is 'no', then, in my view, while sex is possible, problems of 'technique' should be able to take care of themselves.

The best list that I have ever read of what the attributes of the *agape* type of love might be, was written by St Paul in I Corinthians 13:4–7.[2] Nowhere in that list, in any translation that I have ever seen, is there a notion that it is destructive to either oneself or another. I wish they would invent a different word for all that other stuff. (It seems to me that every feature of that list is quite logical and rational; they appear to be violated only when emotions muddy the waters.)

Considering all of this, if I am deemed to be someone who is 'incapable of love', as my mother was the first to say, then perhaps I ought to wear that as yet another badge of honor.

Lest this topic be ended on too gloomy a note, and considering remarks made earlier about cats having many autistic traits,[3] one may suppose that a woman who is capable of loving a cat (and has not tried to make a dog out of it) could conceivably be genuinely quite fond of a highly functioning autistic man.

2   'Love is patient and kind; it is neither jealous, possessive, nor pompous; it is not inflated; it is not rude; it does not seek after its own interest; it is not quick-tempered, nor does it brood over injury; it does not rejoice over evil, but rejoices in the truth; it bears all things, believes all things, hopes all things, and endures all things.'

3   I believe that one intrinsic part of cats' charm is the haughty disdain with which they view the universe.

The Emotional Deficit

When talking to people about autism, this aspect of it has been the most difficult to put across. This is true even when it comes to people who are understanding, open-minded, and even sympathetic. I believe that it must be understood, for I have come to be of the opinion that it is the bedrock characteristic of autism.

This is not some personal hangup. I should like to refer back to my initial discovery and recall two important items. When I first saw that *New Yorker* article, it was a sentence in the subtitle that caught my eye: 'Can an artist make art without feeling it?' When I wrote to Temple Grandin about my discovery, in her reply it was the emotional deficit that she identified as the hallmark of my autism.

It has become my very strong belief that all other autistic traits can be explained in terms of it and, furthermore, it also explains why autistic people are often misdiagnosed with other psychological disabilities, since many outward symptoms are similar, but have different causes.

There is a mathematical analogue to this. Consider any positive number, for instance: 4. What is the square root of that number? In other words, which number, when multiplied by itself, gives us 4? There are *two* correct answers: +2 and -2. Which of them is the one we want?

In like manner, there are sets of ailments, both physical and psychological, in which symptoms are similar, but which are quite different *and require different approaches.* Because of this latter consideration, this is no exercise in intellectual hairsplitting.

Perhaps a medical example is in order. Chicken Pox produces a pervasive rash. So does a bad case of Poison Ivy. To the uncritical observer, they could be confused with one another. Yet they are radically different and they certainly should not be treated with the same procedures.

Earlier, I have compared the emotional deficit with blindness. The physiological similarities are obvious. The eye has a number of mechanisms that take light from some object or other and, through a number of stages, transform it to a visual image recognizable by a person's mind. In like manner, there is a portion of the brain that enables a person to generate and process emotions. (I use the phrase 'generate and process', because I do not 'feel' anything except through my physical senses.)

One difference is that, while the eye is sufficiently formed, at birth, to fulfill its function, the brain takes a number of years to develop fully, or, since it is essentially an electrical system, to 'become wired'. From what I have read, the part of the brain that deals with the intuitive emotions is wired by the age of two.

If any part of the chain that transforms light into an image in the mind comes to malfunction, this transformation does not take place and no image is created. This is what is called 'blindness'. Likewise, a person can be rendered incapable of 'feeling emotions', if that part of the brain either fails to become properly wired or, as happened in my case, becomes unwired. (This is what is meant by 'brain damage'.)

While this physiological effect can, in this manner, be explained quite clearly, understanding it is quite something else. Here is where another important difference with blindness comes into play.

Suppose a sighted person wishes to experience blindness in order to truly understand it (much in the same manner that Parsifal had to feel the king's pain, not just observe it). He or she can, for a day or so, wear those blinders that insomniacs use to block out light. During this time, he or she can experience, first hand, living in the blind person's world of darkness.

What, on the other hand, can an NT person do that would cause him or her to turn off his or her emotions? Every time I have asked this question, the silence that followed clearly implied: 'Nothing'.

The difficulty NT people encounter in coming to grips with even the concept of this has a complementary counterpart in myself. All of my life I have attempted to understand a mysterious motivation for what people say and do. These attempts have met with varying degrees of failure. (For most of that life, I was totally unaware that I never could and never would.)

While I have been able, to a considerable degree, sense some patterns, any underlying basis for those words and actions still escapes me, and always will. I have had to develop, in order to function in society, a list of thou-shalt-nots and thou-musts[1] (what mathematicians call the 'cookbook' approach). No wonder Temple Grandin described herself as 'an anthropologist on Mars'.[2]

---

1   An example of a recent acquisition: when people talk about their divorces, each time 'amicable' is uttered thou must substitute 'acrimonious'.

2   Sacks, Oliver: *op. cit.*

Suppose, on the other hand, a person has suffered no impairment in that part of the brain; it has been properly wired. Yet, because of certain psychological factors, they do not show the emotions that they have and even suppress them. One reason I have been given is that they find these things too painful to bear, and so they deny them. (I have, in an earlier chapter, briefly commented on this.) Can the difference between such a person and a person with the genuine emotional deficit be discerned? The answer is 'no and yes'.

This is not an evasion. In the outward and visible signs, no difference can be detected. However, when one goes into the inward and invisible motivations, the difference becomes clear. These, however, are quite subtle. These symptoms come under the heading of what has come to be called 'sociability'.

The term used often for lack of sociability is 'schizoid'. (I shall use that term, for purposes of brevity, to denote someone who has emotions, but suppresses them.) I will catalog a number of those outward signs (call them 'symptoms') and show why, as I see it, both the autistic and the schizoid person would exhibit them.

(1) Does not seek or enjoy close relationships, including being part of a family: This sort of thing requires bonding on an emotional basis. The autistic person has no emotions with which to bond. The schizoid person shies away from such bonding because it hurts, although he or she might both need and want it very much.

(2) Almost always chooses solitary activities: The autistic person is self-sufficient, and enjoys those activities, joining in group activities only when there is a great personal interest (any bonding is strictly intellectual or aesthetic). The schizoid person chooses those activities because he or she sees group activities as requiring some degree of emotional bonding.

(3) Has little, if any, interest in having a sexual experience with another person: For NT people, there has to be an emotional component to that experience. For the autistic person, unless the partner has aesthetic appeal, only the physical aspect has any importance, and this does not absolutely require a partner (perhaps we can call this 'playing solitaire'). For the schizoid person, the emotional aspect is frightening enough to overcome any physical need, which, for him or her, could be a source of great anxiety.

(From what I have read of the accounts of the autistic, while they might enjoy it very much, they are take-it-or-leave-it people.)

(4) Takes pleasure in few, if any, activities: I, an autistic person, have quite a number of interests, almost all of them being intellectual or aesthetic in nature (I am, whenever possible, a participant, not just an onlooker), and bond first with the activity, then, perhaps, with some other participants. For the schizoid person, individual activities underscore his or her loneliness, while group activities raise the specter of emotional involvement.

(5) Appears indifferent to the praise or criticism of others: The autistic person, lacking emotions, has no feelings to either hurt or massage. (In fact, I actually welcome constructive criticism, seeing it as a learning experience.) For the schizoid person, praise is seen as undeserved, while criticism reinforces his or her bad opinion of himself or herself.

(6) Shows emotional coldness, detachment, or distance: The autistic person has no emotions to show, and, as a result, even when doing kind and generous things, does them in a matter-of-fact way that appears cold, detached, uninvolved, distant, even mechanical. (Given the fact that I cannot grieve, many times I must have seemed to be unfeeling and heartless.) The schizoid person is afraid to show feelings because he or she feels quite vulnerable, and is sure that another will use those expressions of emotion to hurt him or her.

(7) Fantasizes, sometimes to the point of being delusional: I fantasize a lot because I have a good imagination, but also have a strong sense of reality, so I am never delusional and do not confuse fantasy with reality. The heightened sense of reality stems from not bringing any emotional baggage into my evaluation of things. The schizoid person uses fantasy to escape from a painful reality, and sometimes that fantasy becomes his or her own reality (this is when it becomes delusion).

(8) Tends to suspicion: The autistic person does not react to things the way others do, nor does he or she evaluate things the same way, so is considered eccentric; suspiciousness comes from being constantly misinterpreted because of that. The schizoid person

tends to feel that people are about to do him or her harm, so believes the worst about others.

In light of the above, how can the autistic and the schizoid personality be distinguished one from the other? I can think of two ways.

The first is that a schizoid person, because he or she finds personal interaction painful, is loathe to talk about his or her thought or feelings, believing that will underscore his or her vulnerability. An autistic person, who can communicate, will do so freely because he or she sees no reason for not doing so. When I was subject to that unwarranted schizophrenia diagnosis, practitioners with whom I spoke were all amazed at the way I would talk about my thoughts in the most minute detail. (I could never understand their amazement; they asked for information and I gave it.)

While on that subject, psychotherapy and group therapy never did me any good at all. At the group therapy sessions, I was praised for the contributions that I made (all intellectual observations in nature), but could never see any benefit that I got out of it. Psychotherapy is supposed to get one 'in touch with one's feelings' (any of which I do not have). The therapists complained, after a while, that the sessions amounted to little more than social visits, and that I was not contributing. To this day, I have not the vaguest notion what it was I was supposed to be contributing.

As to the second item, I refer back to a previous chapter, in which I wrote that, if someone who looks troubled tells me that everything is OK, I have no way to discern that it means that he or she needs help with a serious problem. As a result, I will leave him or her alone. The schizoid person will do that also, but for a different reason. The distress signal, in that case, is definitely picked up. However, not wanting to add the other person's emotional load to his or her own, he or she will also walk away.

The difference comes in the situation in which the troubled person says, 'I do need help, and here's why.' The schizoid person, for the above reason, will suddenly remember an important appointment, while the emotionless person will ask, 'What can I do to help?' Unfortunately, to a person who does not understand the emotional deficit, that help will appear to be given in a cold, aloof manner.

I devoted a great deal of space to what it would take for a successful marriage between an autistic man and an NT woman. The question came up during one episode of *Star Trek*. It involved Mr. Spock, for whom the only motivation is 'It was the logical thing to do'. (That is just about mine also.) An interesting digression is *à propos* here.

I have taken Temple Grandin's characterization of herself and turned it around. Since I do live on Earth, and am clearly outnumbered, I call myself 'an anthropologist *from* Mars'. Also, a friend of mine, who knows of my autism, told me that, when we first met (when neither of us knew), from the way I spoke and acted, she had to wonder whether or not I was an alien. In addition, a woman, also with AS, whom I know from the Internet, emailed me a copy of her homepage. The title was 'Oops! Wrong planet!' Another would sign off her posts with, 'Diagonally parked in a parallel universe'.

If, by observing the way we operate, we come across as, if not from outer space, at least a different species, it is quite understandable. An appropriate Biblical quotation is Isaiah 55:8 'For my thoughts are not your thoughts, nor are your ways my ways'.

Conversely, the ways of the NT are no small mystery to me, or others like me, especially in that they often violate logic and rationality. On more than one occasion, in my thoughts, I have paraphrased Shakespeare's Puck: 'Lord, what fools these earthlings be!'[3] But, as I said, this is a digression.

In her autobiography,[4] Temple Grandin says that Spock is her favorite character on television. In the episode in question, Spock was asked why his parents (a Vulcan father and a human mother) had married each other. When Spock asked his father, his response was, 'At the time, it seemed to be the logical thing to do'. The writers neglected to have Spock ask his mother the same question. Perhaps they realized that her answer could not be encapsulated in a one-liner.

At the beginning of this chapter, I said that there was a danger in misunderstanding the nature of autism, in that an inappropriate therapy might be used (which might actually be helpful to the schizoid person). This is generally popularized as 'straightening out his or her emotional turmoil'. This approach is akin to trying to find the proper eyeglass prescription for someone who is blind.

I started this chapter by noting that this is an extremely difficult concept for NT people to even comprehend, much less grasp. I guess that this is the reason many professionals[5] soft-pedal this aspect of autism when dealing with the parents of autistic children. They must feel, with a certain

3   *A Midsummer Night's Dream*: Act III, Scene 2.
4   Grandin, Temple: *op. cit.*, p.131.
5   When I use the word 'professional', in connection with the autistic, I refer to psychiatrists, psychologists, therapists, and educators.

amount of justification, that bringing up something so seemingly outlandish might damage their credibility with those parents. Perhaps my credibility in this matter might be somewhat greater. I can only hope.

Self-Compensating?

In the not too distant past, the media took note of a ten-year-old autistic boy who wandered into the swamps that surround Eglin Air Force Base in Florida's northwest panhandle. Those swamps are used by the Army to train Rangers and Special Forces. As a result, those taking the training, as well as their cadre, were pressed into service to look for the boy. They found him, four days later, seemingly none the worse for wear.

What enabled him to survive such an ordeal so well? Ironically, it was very likely the autistic traits that got him into that perilous situation in the first place.

In an earlier chapter, I mentioned that autistic people sometimes have two characteristics that could possibly prove dangerous: lack of fear of real physical dangers, and a high threshold for both pain and discomfort. (I happen to have both of these.)

Because he did not sense that swamp as being a potentially dangerous place, he satisfied his normal ten-year-old curiosity by exploring this strange new place. He did not bother leaving a trail or tell anyone where he was going because he saw no danger in 'being lost'.

Once in the swamp, and not knowing how to return home, he was faced with deprivation of food and water, and numerous unpleasant fauna such as snakes and alligators. Hunger and thirst did not bother him because of his high threshold for discomfort, and if he scratched himself or stubbed his toe, he did not feel the sharp pain that any other boy might have felt. When he saw snakes or alligators, he did not see them as a source of danger, so he did not panic. Since he did not, neither did they, so they did not attack him.

When he was found, he probably did not quite understand the fuss that everyone was making out of the incident. This might be important for the parents of an autistic child to understand; he or she does not see the world the way his or her parents do, so what disturbs the parents greatly bothers the child not at all. In such a situation, the parent must choose very carefully which type of incident about which to make a big deal.

This phenomenon manifests itself in a number of other situations, mostly of a social nature.

All of my life, I have been an outsider, never feeling part of any group. Even when I do things that are clearly group activities, such as singing in a chorus, I am an individual doing what the others are doing, to be sure, but, nevertheless, as an individual. Other people like to discuss 'relationships' but, because these involve emotional considerations, they might as well be talking about their vacations on the far side of the moon.

I, therefore, by default, exclude myself from most people's conversations. Even when I do talk about interactions between people, it is invariably from an ethical point of view. This, I am sure, carries with it an air of aloofness that, though inadvertent, is perceived as intentional by others.

One aspect of this that deserves special mention is how it affects my religious practices. My church, especially at the Eucharistic celebration, stresses the idea of doing things communally. (Many parishes refer to themselves as 'a Catholic community'.) I have never felt that sort of thing. I did not convert to obtain a sense of 'belonging'. When I attend mass, it is as though no one else is there but the celebrant and myself. This has made it very easy for me to attend mass anywhere in the world and not feel 'out of place'.

For the NT, from what I have observed, being an outsider is a traumatic situation, causing great pain. I, on the other hand, have never been bothered in the slightest by this, being quite content with any resulting solitude.

For as far back as I can remember, I always had my own set of values (which were invariably arrived at by intellectual criteria), and, as such, did not hesitate to question the values of others if they seemed to me to be illogical. (One example is the questioning of my family's values that eventually led to my adoption of Catholicism.)

Adolescents enforce on each other a much more draconian conformity than their parents ever enforced on them. (Oddly, they claim that, in so doing, they are asserting their 'independence'. It always seemed to me that they only traded one dependence for another.) They do not suffer nonconformity gladly. An outsider, such as myself, is snubbed socially. I have seen many an NT nonconformist made to suffer cruelly. Since I had no feelings to hurt, this also did not cause me any grief.

I had mentioned earlier that I do experience the survival-type emotions: fear and anger. So do the NT, but, for them, like their other emotions, they are persistent; mine are purely situational. Fear does not become a phobia, nor does anger turn into hatred. When the incident that provoked those emotions passes, so does the feeling. I carry neither torches nor grudges.

There is an example of this dating to the age of thirteen. My mother had divorced her second husband (I wrote earlier about my experiences with him). Since I was clearly a loner (a cause of great concern to my family; they always wondered 'what they were going to do with me'), my mother attributed that to what had passed during that period. At the time, Freudian psychoanalysis was deemed to be good for whatever ails you, so she put me into analysis.

During one session, the analyst asked me to tell her about my relationship with my stepfather. After recounting a number of details, she said to me, 'You are very polite'. I was taken aback, since I was usually deemed inconsiderate of others' feelings. I asked her what on earth she meant by that. She told me that, when other patients told a story like that, they would seethe with anger.

I could not understand what her problem was. As far as I was concerned, she had asked for information, and I had given it to her. Living with my stepfather was unquestionably an unpleasant experience but, once it was over, it was as though it were ancient history in another galaxy.

Since the autistic (others with whom I have corresponded as well as myself) appear to have lost the intuitive emotions, but retain the survival ones, it occurred to me that there might be two emotion centers in the brain, one for each type. The intuitive center would have to be vulnerable, while that for the survival type would have to be protected.

Recent neurological research has borne this out. The survival center is in mid-brain. If anything gets to that, the rest of the brain is likely gone before that happens. The intuitive center is in one of the temporal lobes. These are both exposed and vulnerable.

There is a phenomenon that is the bane of all kinds of health practitioners: denial. This can be defined as a refusal to face facts and act on them, mostly by pretending that those facts are not really true, when one has to know that they are.

(The best example of this sort of thing in literature is to be found in Book VI of Virgil's Æneid. When he goes into the Underworld, just before crossing the Styx, Æneas comes across the ghost of his steersman Palinurus, who lies unburied in an inaccessible place. He is thus unable to cross the Styx and find rest. He begs Æneas to use his influence, as a living man, to get an exception made for him. The Sybil, who is Æneas' guide, reproaches Palinurus, reminding him that such a thing is not possible under any circumstances. Palinurus had hoped for the impossible as though it might just be possible.[1] Isn't that denial?)

Because I have such a strong sense of reality, and do not bring irrelevant emotions into my decisions, I do not indulge in this sort of thing; I do what is the logical thing to do. This does not to say that I have not made bad decisions. Those, however, were invariably made because the information on which I acted was either erroneous or incomplete.

I have gone into great detail in these last two chapters to point out that the difference between the autistic and the NT is one of substance, not accidents. This discovery has helped me to not only realize that nature, while it deprived me of something others have, has erected defenses against any number of things that, for the NT, would cause serious psychological problems.

By the same token, I have been able to come to understand what it is like, for the NT, to have to deal with someone like me. This has enabled me not only to accept myself for what I am, but also to accept those around me for what they are, even if most of those differences are incomprehensible to me. Kipling said it best with a couplet from *If*:

> If you can trust yourself when all men doubt you,
> But make allowance for their doubting too.

The parents of young autistic children, verbal or not, would do well to ponder that.

I have remarked in an earlier chapter that what I had thought to be great strength of character (resisting peer pressure in my teens, etc.), in light of this, was actually the result of my autism compensating for my social shortcomings. If one does not fear danger, then one cannot be considered a hero for facing it.

Yet, I am reminded of the biggest fear that I do have, and that is uncertainty. While society's usual penalties for the loner and the outsider did not bother me, there was one thing that did. My family and friends were constantly after me to warm up, lighten up, come out of my shell, and so on, and to stop being so cold, distant, detached, unemotional, and so forth, as if I could do that simply by deciding to.

I did not know that there was no way I could be different from what I was; I could only, to live in the world, work around it. This ignorance

---

1   Virgil was able to make this quite explicit, since Latin is an inflected language, by the sequence of tenses.

resulted in a great uncertainty that they might possibly be right, and that, somehow, I could possibly will to be less asocial, if only I would try. The fact that, for most of my life, I was able to endure the fear that was fed by this uncertainty, perhaps might indicate that I did have sources of strength within me for which I have not heretofore given myself sufficient credit.

Our Own Country

As I have mentioned before, I have always felt like an 'outsider'. Even during the times that I have not been explicitly conscious of that, this was something that was made plain to me by others.

For example, as a teenager, one of my contemporaries referred to me as 'an eccentric phony'. While I might have agreed with the adjective, I was nonplussed by the noun. I had always, to use an old bromide, said what I meant and meant what I said. As a child, I had told many lies as a survival tactic, but I soon recognized that I was no good at that at all, so I told the truth instinctively, realizing, if only pragmatically, that the consequences of telling the truth were invariably less than those of being caught in a lie.

I was told by someone, when in my mid twenties: 'Ed, the trouble with you is that you're not a mixer; you're not part of the group.' It is not that I did not try. Not being aware, at that time, that I simply did not think as others did, I could never understand why virtually all of my attempts to be 'part of the group' came a cropper.

When I got my first big promotion at work, my new manager told me that I would have gotten it much sooner, except for the fact that I was considered 'unpredictable'. That baffled me. I did not know how to answer that. Given how I thought and how I made decisions, I believed myself to be totally predictable, almost to the point of boredom. But, at that time, how could I have explained the differences in our thought processes, when I myself had not the faintest notion that they were different?

In a lighter vein, shortly after that, one of my co-workers gave me what I think of today as the best compliment I have ever gotten. He told me that I couldn't even be filed under 'miscellaneous'.

Quite recently an incident occurred at which I was able to be amused, knowing, at long last, of the fact and the nature of my autism. I had been called for jury duty, and was chosen to be on a panel for some minor criminal case.[1]

After hearing the testimony and seeing the physical evidence, I realized that there were major flaws in the prosecution's case, mostly due to what was a careless police investigation. (Mathematically, these could be called 'gaps in logic'.) The judge obviously believed as I did; before we could even begin our deliberations, he granted a defense motion for a directed verdict of acquittal.

Before going home, I saw the prosecutor in the courthouse hallway. I approached him and wanted to tell him about the logic gaps that I had noted. Before I could say much more than 'hello', he said to me: 'I had some concern about allowing you to be on the panel. I was worried about you; you're different.'

I let it go at that.

From the above, 'different' is one of the minor pejoratives that have been applied to me, but it is the most to the point. I have always been different, but, until recently, have not known why. I might point out that other examples of 'different' people are serial killers and those who disrobe in the street during rush hour. When I use the word 'different', I mean those whose appearance or traits may be at variance with the population at large, but who also manage to not run afoul of the law. (These laws would include those against disturbing the peace or creating a public nuisance.)

Being different, in this sense, also implies having values that are not those held by society at large, and having social penalties exacted by that society for doing that. (Hate groups, which could technically fit this definition, have to be excluded, for obvious reasons. But, I suspect, they are often just saying out loud what more respectable people are thinking, so their greatest offense might really be bad public relations.)

This is an idea that plays an important rôle in Wagner's opera Die Walküre.[2] Hunding (the villain) has just discovered that Siegmund (the hero), to whom he has just unknowingly offered his hospitality, is a member of a family who, in Hunding's society, are considered outcasts.

---

1   For those unfamiliar with tthe American jury system, before a person is placed on a jury, he or she must pass the *voir-dire* examination, in which the judge and lawyers for both sides get to question him or her, in order to assure that he or she will try the case in an impartial manner.

2   *The Valkyrie.*

The way he characterizes them is as a people who do not prize the things that others prize, and that this is why they are hated by all,[3] including him.

On the Internet, I have encountered many autistic people who talked about having to cope with being 'different' in a society that does not suffer that gladly. (I find it interesting that human cultures that claim to prize individualism should also look upon expressions of individuality with reactions that vary from suspicion to hostility.) I posted the following, after seeing a great deal of that.

When I was an adolescent, the film director Jean Renoir (son of Pierre-Auguste, the impressionist painter) made a movie called *The River*. It took place in India, shortly after World War II, before the end of the British raj.[4] Among the characters were a war veteran, who had lost a leg, and a young woman of mixed British and Hindu parentage.

They both felt completely left out. For the veteran, it was because, at that time, since there were few opportunities for those with disabilities, he saw no real productive future for himself. For the young woman, it was because, although both her parents were upper-class, she was not accepted in the social circles of either the British rulers or caste Hindus.

In one scene, the young man lamented his condition and wished he were some place where his disability would not be a handicap. The young woman rhetorically asked him where there might be a country where all men had a wooden leg.

This started a thread[5] among autistic people about their experiences in being treated as outsiders, and even, in some cases, as outcasts. The subject line, on all the messages was: Our Own Country.

There is a song, familiar to many classical music lovers, in which these sentiments, that I saw time and again, are vividly illustrated. It is *Der Wanderer*[6] by Franz Schubert. In the poem, by Schmidt von Lübeck, the singer laments that he is a stranger everywhere, and asks where his beloved country might be, the country where every person speaks the singer's language.

Somehow, I have managed to function in society, and even adapt to it. Though I have had a few hospitalizations due to that schizophrenia misdiagnosis, I have never been institutionalized. Nor have I ever been

---

3   The original text is: 'Ich weiss ein wildes Geschlecht, nicht heilig ist ihm, was andern hehr: verhasst ist es allen und mir.'
4   Colonial rule.
5   A series of back-to-back Internet messages on the same topic.
6   *The Wanderer.*

incarcerated or had to rely on public assistance. This is all while being an outsider, even in activities in which I have been deeply involved.

In many ways, this was due to a very fortunate confluence of circumstances. I owe it, in a way, to Nikita Khrushchev and also to the coterie of anti-intellectuals with which President Eisenhower surrounded himself. This requires no small amount of explanation.

The contempt in which intellectuality was held at that time beggars description. (Adlai Stevenson, the twice Democratic candidate for President, was derisively called an 'egghead'.) The Secretary of Defense justified cutting the budget for basic research because, as he said, the Army shouldn't be looking into why potatoes turn brown when they're fried. The personnel director of a major corporation was quoted as saying that they had a policy against hiring 'bookworms or other oddballs'. He said, 'We'd much rather have a Deke than a Phi Beta Kappa'.

Then, the Soviet Union managed to put into space the first artificial satellite, *Sputnik*. Everyone believed that our national escutcheon had been besmirched. How did they ever get so far ahead of us technologically? We had to catch up, and even overtake them! From that point on, people, who had the knowledge and skills such as I was soon to have, found themselves in great demand, even if they were 'different'.

(Ironically, it was because, in some respects, we *were* ahead of the Soviet Union that this happened. Our scientists and engineers had managed to miniaturize our thermonuclear warheads so that we did not need a very powerful rocket in order to deliver them. The Soviets, on the other hand, in order to deliver their cumbersome warheads, needed a missile sufficiently powerful to also be able to put a satellite into an earth orbit. The nation's leaders did not know this, nor, disdaining anything cerebral, did they care. It was a total knee-jerk reaction, born of ignorance and false pride.)

It was this that enabled me to be an outsider without becoming an outcast. Had that incident not happened, and had the intellectual climate *not* changed, there is the strong possibility that, even with my graduate study in physics and mathematics, I too could have ended up sleeping in a cardboard box underneath a bridge.

I have written earlier about my fear of uncertainty and how this exacerbated my bewilderment at not being able to 'fit in'. Because of this, the discovery of who and what I was turned out to be the cure for whatever was ailing me. I was able, at long last, to confront my limitations while remaining cognizant of my abilities. One result is that I have, ironically, become, much more of an extrovert than I had been before. I found a greater ease in dealing with people, because I knew how I was *not* able to interact with them.

The Bible[7] says the truth will make you free; it does not say that it will make you happy. However, if you are really free, you can make your own happiness. Again according to that passage in the Bible, before the truth can make you free, you must *know* the truth. This does not imply merely seeing or hearing it, but also understanding and accepting it.

There is a story that is rather stupid, but it has a point that illustrates what is, from where I look at the world, a major source of people's unhappiness.

A man was on a luxury cruise when the ship suddenly fell apart and sank. He managed to get to the surface and grabbed onto a piece of debris to keep himself afloat. In the distance he saw an island, and managed to get to the shore. He looked down the beach and saw that there was another survivor. He walked toward that person. As he got closer, he saw that it was a woman. When he got really close, he saw that it was a world-famous supermodel. (Fill in the name yourself.) It only took about a half-hour for them to discover that they were the only survivors, and that the island was otherwise deserted.

After they had been there for a few weeks, during a lull in the conversation, he asked her, 'Would you do me a big favor? It may sound strange, but it would mean a lot to me if you would do it.' 'Sure,' she said, 'as long as it's not too much trouble'. He said, 'Remember that suit and hat I was wearing when I came ashore? Would you put them on?' She thought that this indeed was strange, but harmless, so she did as he asked. He continued, 'Would you rub some charcoal from the campfire under your nose, like it's a moustache?' She did so. 'Now,' he said, 'would you walk around the island along the beach?' She nodded and started walking.

He started walking along the beach in the opposite direction. After a short time, they came within sight of each other. When this happened, he started running toward her, waving his arms, and shouting, 'Hey there, guy! You'll never guess who I've been having sex with!'

What is the point to this admittedly stupid story? No matter what people have, or how much they have, they cannot seem to enjoy it unless others are jealous of it.

Advertizing does often take advantage of the notion that the envy of others is what people seem to prize, if not most of all at least very highly.

---

7   John 8:32

Given that, someone whose value system does not include that, would be considered 'different' to the point of being an outsider.

This attitude must be quite common, since virtually all advertising is geared toward that. So often, the message is, 'If you buy this, all your friends and relatives will be green with envy'.

It baffles me how anyone could do this as his or her primary pursuit of happiness. One will never have enough, because there is always someone who has more, and one will have to be jealous of that person. Even if one is the 'richest' in the world, then one has to live with the constant fear of losing it, and thus having less than others.

Gershwin's Porgy eloquently points that out. Mother Teresa's life was a witness to the fact that one does not need material possessions, fame, family, or even sex, if one has discovered a purpose to one's life. If one does not have such a purpose, then one can never have enough of those other things.

This is not to imply that one should unreasonably deprive oneself of any of those things as a way of 'building character'. (That could be said to border on masochism.) This should only be done for two reasons. The first is if these things would interfere with the purpose one has found for one's life. The other is if acquiring those things can only be done by depriving others.

It is my belief that gratuitous asceticism and hedonism may very well be opposite sides of the same coin. However, believing that one's life cannot have any purpose or meaning has got to be, in spite of what or how much one possesses, the ultimate in surrender.

This autobiography began with a quotation from Alexander Pope. He was asked by the Prince of Wales to compose something that could be used as identification on the collar of one of his dogs. The couplet he wrote eloquently satirizes the desire to arouse the envy of others:

> I am His Highness' dog at Kew.
> Pray tell me, sir, whose dog are you?

In that regard, I have to consider myself a disciple of Giovanni Bernadone and Gautama Siddhartha. Those are their real names, by which hardly anybody knows them.

Giovanni was the son of an extremely wealthy businessman, who wanted his son to continue in his business. When the father got his son so involved, young Giovanni was appalled at the extreme poverty and horrid working conditions of his father's workers. He could not see himself as wanting to be enriched by such things. He then contemplated the Gospel message of how God has placed in the world enough, so that all creatures could have all that they might need in order to lead happy and productive lives. His father was enraged, so Giovanni renounced his family and spent his life living as a poor man and working among the poor.

While his father was local, his mother was French. As a result, the boys he grew up with gave him the nickname 'Frenchy'. In Italian, that is *Francesco*. He is known as St Francis of Assisi.

(It is interesting to note that the habit worn by Franciscan friars was originally the garment commonly worn by poor men in the thirteenth century.)

Gautama, as a prince, was also born to power and privilege. He, when he had reached adulthood, saw how empty the lives were of those who shared in his advantages, and compared that with the misery and poverty of most people. He came to a conclusion that was, if nothing else, quite logical. One only needs so much in order to live; everything else is optional. Beyond what is needed for survival, if what one has exceeds what one wants, the result is happiness. If what one wants exceeds what one has, the result is unhappiness.

(This is not to say that one should choose living at the barest subsistence level. Perhaps it could be summed up by asking oneself a series of questions about personal acquisitions. 'Do I need this?' 'If not, do I really want it, or do I only want others' envy?' 'If I get it, will I be depriving someone else of something important?' 'If not, can I get it ethically and responsibly?' There is an important aspect of 'ethically and "responsibly'. One should not, to satisfy a want, deprive another of a need.)

He taught this to anyone who would listen, leaving his former life and living as a pauper. He was seen as someone who had discovered the secret of a fulfilling life, even by those who could not bring themselves to escape the quest for more and greater riches. Because of this, he was called 'The Enlightened One', which, in Sanskrit, is *Buddha*.

One often hears and sees appeals for 'tolerance'. They are, by their nature, pleas on behalf of those who are different from the majority, whether because of race, ethnicity, religion, tastes in music or other entertainment, philosophical outlook, social or economic class, or even disability.[8] They all, I believe, miss the point. They urge us to overlook the differences, and concentrate instead on 'how alike we all are'.

---

8   Perhaps 'mood disorders' could be listed among these.

This is sweeping the essence of the tolerance problem under the rug. After viewing as much of my past life as I am able to remember, I know how different I, and others like me, are. According to correspondence I have had with other autistic people, some have been able to adapt better than others. Yet, I know that my differences cannot be papered over; I have had to deal with them as best I could, mostly in ignorance of what those differences were. Perhaps, instead of dwelling on similarities, people should be asking themselves: 'What is wrong with being different?'

Retrospect

If I had these insights into myself from the time of my youth, perhaps I would never have married, or even had more than a casual date. I would very likely have tried to become a scholar-priest. (A late good friend of mine, who knew about my autism, had told me that I would have been very good at that.)

I know that one can be a scholar without being a priest, but, as a priest, nobody would constantly be on your case about finding a nice woman and getting married. In fact, before I met the woman I married, shortly after my discharge from the Army, I was giving serious thought to becoming a Jesuit.[1] This gave me a very good line to use in our early arguments: 'I should have gone ahead and become a Jesuit'. She made me quit using that line, on one occasion, by saying to me, 'You're not cunning enough to be a Jesuit'.

(This, of course, would have involved living by myself and keeping to myself. However, I have always found that to be extremely easy, even when surrounded by people, or even in close quarters with them. No wonder; my autism notwithstanding, I have had so much practice in doing this that I could not help but be good at it.)

What I wrote earlier, about *philos* being the only kind of love of which I am capable, bears strongly on these last points. Even if I should become, given my limitations, quite fond of a woman, 'I love you with my whole head', probably would not come across as very romantic. Yet, in Greek, 'Se phileo'[2] can be said by a cerebral person, with all the intensity an emotional person uses to say, 'Se agapao'.[3] Perhaps even more.

I must have been no small disappointment to those, especially in my family, who may have depended on me for some emotional rapport in their lives, but, as much as I might regret this, I know now that this is something

---

1   A Roman Catholic order of priests. One of their areas of specialization is the reconciliation of science and religion.

2   Σε φιλεω 'I love you' in the *philos* sense

3   Σε α γαπαω 'I love you' in the *agape* sense.

that I could not have changed by any act of the will. This is, of course, very cold comfort to those who may have depended on me that way, perhaps for the better part of their lives.

In a way, I can understand and sympathize with some of the epithets that come with my type of personality: 'unfeeling', 'self-centered', 'cold fish', and so on. Everybody has always commented on how good I have been at so many endeavors. However, if I were asked to name my biggest failure, it would have to be: not being able to give at least one woman happiness with my constant, close companionship over the long haul.

What I have Tried to do Here

I have to begin this chapter by stating what I have *not* tried to do here. A great amount of space has been devoted to my views on topics too numerous to list. I was not trying to make any converts. I could not, even if I wanted to, because I am an explainer and not a persuader.

My intent was to explain how things are perceived and how opinions are formed by the autistic mind. In particular, how such perceptions and opinions take can place independent of any intuitive emotions.[1]

I wrote, at the beginning, that I wanted others to know me better. Other than having made such an easy swipe of the title from the autobiography of Cardinal Newman, the word *apologia* has a special significance. In a technical sense, it is Latin for defense of what one has done or said. Indeed, the dialogue of Plato in which Socrates defends himself before the Athenian court is called the *Apology*.

Yet, Socrates did not feel that he needed to either defend himself or apologize for what he had said. Instead, he tried to *explain* to the people of Athens what he was all about. I hope that I have had more success than he had.[2]

I hope that I have been able to give some idea of what autism is all about, because it has to be the most misunderstood disability there is. One HFA person on the Internet said, 'It is not a normal disability'. This should be kept in mind by those responsible for forming government programs that deal with autism.

A common term used is *the autistic spectrum*. This implies a variation, but also a common trait. I have devoted an entire chapter to what I believe is the common trait: the emotional deficit. The variability comes in the form of other disabilities that may have nothing to do with this, but which may be found among many of the autistic, for example, ADD, OCD, sensory

---

1 Sometimes, tongue-in-cheek, I call this the 'Vulcan's eye view'.
2 For, among other things, encouraging young people to question (not just contradict) society's values, and causing people to examine the logical consequences of their beliefs, he was condemned to death.

overload, and so on. There are those with sociability problems, limited communication ability, or learning disabilities who are not autistic.

The way I think of that, uses the mathematical terminology of set theory. The emotional deficit is the trait common to all elements. I have called AS 'the highest functioning form of autism', so HFA is a subset of autism and AS is a subset of HFA.

I should like to have shown that it is possible for those without autism to communicate with those having the high functioning variety, and how they can do it.

Also, in my admittedly enigmatic account of my school experiences, and how I have learned, I hope that educators might find some clues as to how help autistic children learn more effectively. To encapsulate the steps in both my learning journey and my adaptation to the world: art gave me a refuge from the world, music made me want to get involved with the world, and mathematics made me want to reach out to the world.

I would like my self-explanation to reach parents, so that they might recognize early in life the signs of an autistic child and get that child the necessary help instead of merely dismissing him or her as an antisocial brat. (If the provider diagnoses the child as autistic, and then proceeds to treat him or her for emotional problems, the parent should look elsewhere.) Another thing the parent should be aware of is, if he or she is high functioning, this child could also grow up totally aware of himself or herself and, thus, be able to plan his or her life prudently.

The final group I should like to address consists of mental health professionals. This perhaps might accomplish two things. The first is that they might not make a faulty diagnosis and subject the patient to what I had to endure as a result of mine. (One thing that must be avoided is having autism become the new fashionable default diagnosis.) The second is that they might realize that, just as autism is not mental retardation, neither is it, in the classic sense, mental or emotional illness, and, as a result, should not be treated as such.

Conclusion

In conclusion, looking at myself as being autistic was as big a surprise to me as it might be to anyone who reads this. At first, I did experience some difficulty coming to grips with the idea even after I had finished that *New Yorker* article. One usually thinks of an autistic person strictly in terms of someone for whom no communication channel exists to the world outside himself. At best, if he is a *savant*, one thinks of Raymond in the movie *The Rain Man* who, as my youngest son pointed out, 'had to be led around by the hand'.

Under no circumstances do people usually think of the autistic as being articulate.

I guess that I do have to thank God for the many high functioning gifts that I do have. Otherwise, I might easily have been like the autistic types I described just above. As it is, I have been able to be a productive member of society, and have two generations of posterity so beautiful and bright as to make any man want to believe in heredity. Also, the gifts that I have been given have made me, in spite of all disappointments and setbacks, able to enjoy life to an extent that few others seem to have been able to duplicate.

This joy that has filled my life due to my intellectual and aesthetic pursuits has more than made up for any joys that I may have missed from my lack of emotional involvement with people. Without it my life would really have been empty.

All of this was underscored, before I realized that I was autistic, by a conversation I had in early 1995, just before I read the *New Yorker* article. In a long lull during one of the *Flying Dutchman* performances (our presence was not required on stage at that time) I chatted with one of the women supernumeraries. We got to talking about the social life of adolescents and young adults. I mentioned to her that I had not dated when in high school, and said that I probably might have missed out on a lot of pleasure. She replied, 'You were probably also spared a lot of pain'.

Epilogue

I have written earlier about how the discovery of my autism has improved my quality of life by enabling me both to understand myself and to explain myself to others, who, for the most part, have accepted me as I have been able to accept myself (once they had been able to absorb certain concepts which, before this, had been totally foreign to them).

The frosting on the cake, or the cherry on top, or whatever one wants to call it, has been that I have been able to make a positive difference in the lives of others. How that came about was quite unpremeditated.

As background, following the failure of my marriage (which, as I have mentioned above, could be laid at the door of our joint ignorance of my autism), I was faced with the question of what to do with my life. My existing activities (such as the Florida Philharmonic Chorus and volunteer work in the election campaign of 1996) did not begin to consume my now-available time.

(Later, I did find other volunteer activities, but they are unrelated, other than that they enabled me to help other people without having to get involved with them personally.)

I tried to dip one big toe into the social stream, and discovered that not one thing had changed since my adolescence. All of the game-playing, duplicity, posturing, caginess, and jockeying for position were still alive and well. I had opted out of the whole business as a teenager and was quite prepared to do so again. In fact, the knowledge that I took solitude better than most made that quite easy.

(The posturing is what has always intrigued me the most. I have come to the inescapable conclusion that sex is the only form of entertainment in which the performers are allowed to write their own reviews.)

This is when a friend of mine, who had been quite supportive during the unraveling process, told me that she had a piano tuner who had an autistic son. The boy, I was told, was unable to communicate. She gave me the tuner's phone number and, after a while, I called him hoping to acquire additional insights as a result of our talk.

He told me that he had been quite upset by somewhat bizarre recent behavior on the part of his son. The experts on autism that he had consulted could offer no explanation that made sense to him. I was somewhat curious and asked him to give me the details.

He said that his son was physically hurting himself (the expression that the father used was 'self-abusive behavior'). He tried to determine if there was a physical problem involved, but kept getting the lazy-doctor diagnosis: psychosomatic.

He finally took the boy to New York City, where a local gastro-enterologist found an intestinal blockage, which is quite painful, even given the high pain threshold of autistic people. The condition was treated, cleared up, and the bad behavior went away. He was mystified, as were the professionals.

I gave him the required disclaimer to the effect that I was certifiably *not* an expert in the field of autism, but offered to share with him an explanation that I could garner from two sources. One was knowledge gotten from study of autism, which I felt, given how recently I had gotten into the subject, had to be beggared by that of the experts. The other was introspection which, as I mentioned in the Prologue, practically bristles with unreliability.

I told him that, since he was suffering great pain, could not talk to anyone about it, and had come to believe that nobody could or would relieve that pain, he was experiencing the only emotions that he could: fear and anger. The anger mounted until it boiled over, in which case he turned that anger against himself, as the autistic are wont to do. Of course, once the pain was relieved, the anger subsided and the self-abusive behavior stopped.

That piano tuner initially had a hard time believing that, because it involved ways of thinking and behaving that were foreign to him, but commonplace to the autistic. However, after he had accepted these things, he told me that I had given him the only explanation, of what had happened to his son, that made any sense to him. He thanked me profusely for that, saying that it had set his mind at ease.

Following that experience, it occurred to me that this might be no isolated incident, but that what I had done for the piano tuner, I could also do for other parents of non-communicating autistic children. I obtained, from a list of local resources for autistic children, the names and telephone numbers of some support groups for parents of autistic children.

I contacted the group leaders, told them what I had been able to do for the piano tuner, and suggested that I might be of similar assistance to members of their groups. They invited me to attend their meetings and, thus far, the results have been very encouraging. The parents involved were quite enthusiastic and asked me to continue coming.

It appeared to me that the lion's share of the research is geared toward helping the children learn, with not much going into helping parents understand what is going on inside their children. But then, the professionals do not seem to know that much either. (They cannot be faulted for this, since it involves concepts that, to some, border on the bizarre.) This is where an autistic person who can communicate could be quite valuable.

I am aware of the fact that there are any number of variations in the autistic but, as I wrote earlier, the trait that they all share in common is the emotional deficit. Any other problems depend on what other parts of the brain have been damaged. Thus, my assumption is that the way I think and the ways in which I react to things are the same as other autistic people, with the important exception being that I am able to talk about it.

I approached this with some trepidation because I did not want to appear to professionals to be treading on their turf. This apprehension was dealt with by me via a mechanism I have used before. Note that, in earlier chapters, I employed an analogy between someone who is autistic but high functioning and someone who is blind, in order to examine how NT people could interact with such autistic persons.

In this case, I considered another analogy: a physicist who is studying the structure and behavior of atoms. In much the same manner as the inability of most autistic people to communicate impedes the professional researchers' ability to analyze autistic subjects, the physicist, for all his or her knowledge and expertise, is up against phenomena such as the uncertainty principle in getting at the atom.

Yet, I believed that, if a single atom could talk, it could teach the most eminent physicist quite a bit about quantum mechanics. I approached my psychiatrist (obviously himself a professional) with this notion. He set my mind at ease by telling me, 'When it comes to what goes on inside an autistic person, *you're the professor.*'

The work that I did with these parents' support groups came to the attention of the staff of a local school that specializes in teaching young autistic people (mostly non-communicating). I was invited to talk to teachers and therapists at workshops that they periodically hold.

This is where the trepidation to which I referred above came into play once more. I was convinced that, with every point that I brought up, one of those professionals would quote some study in some learned journal that totally contradicted me. Quite the opposite; many of them told me that they would tailor their methods to what I had revealed to them. I felt an awesome responsibility.

My friend, who told me to contact her piano tuner, showed me how to access autism-related list services[1] on the Internet. This made it possible for me to do worldwide what I had been doing locally.

The reaction that I got from those I contacted on the information superhighway is quite relevant to remarks that I had made earlier: that I wanted to give some idea of how the world looks through autistic eyes, and that I was apprehensive (my last doctor's remark notwithstanding) about any assertion that I might be an 'expert' on autism. After all, my knowledge of autism in general, and of its application to me in particular, only goes back to early 1995, and I am a certifiable expert only on me.

In addition to remarks and comments that I made in response to posts, I also shared with people a briefer version of my life story than I have given here. There were two types of recipients whose own responses helped me to realize that I had indeed come upon the truth about myself.

From parents, I got replies similar to that which I got from the piano tuner: that I had given them new insights into their autistic children. Some parents showed what I had written to their high-functioning children, who then told them that I had described just the way they felt.

But, it was the responses that I got from adult AS and HFA people themselves that were the most telling. While they did note a number of differences that they had with me, they not only attested to their similarities with me, but also told me of words and phrases, that I had used, that fit them and their own situations perfectly. One was the *philos* type of love; another was my concept of a 'dry hole' as opposed to a 'wall'.

I cannot leave this topic without mentioning that, in this last group, I came upon a number of high-powered intellects. Even when we disagreed, the clarity of their thinking was something rare indeed.

Writing about what being able to do this has meant to me is quite difficult. I imagine that it would come easy to someone with an emotional capability (but then, such a person could not have done this). As it is, I have had to think long and hard and to weigh practically every word.

Imagine dipping your hand into a bowl of water and then withdrawing it. If the hole that is left in the water would be a measure of the difference

---

1   For those unfamiliar with the Internet, when one posts a message to a list service, it is automatically forwarded to all of the subscribers. There was no cost in subscribing to the ones I dealt with.

in the world had you not lived, that must be a rather depressing thought, from either an emotional or a logical standpoint.

The help that I seem to have given to those parents has shown me that I could make a difference in the lives of others, not in spite of my condition, but because of it. It has made me believe that I am part of something larger than myself. Furthermore, it has brought home to me that one need not take formal vows and wear distinctive dress in order to have a vocation.

I believe now that any question of whether or not I could become close to anyone on a personal basis, has been rendered irrelevant. This is actually a plus for me since even those who have found my company quite interesting and enjoyable have never 'warmed' up to me.

This is probably because of a popular conception of emotions as being 'warm' while logic is thought of as 'cold'. Is this a fair assessment? I do not think so. I have always seen logic as the indispensable tool in determining the morally right thing to do, which, given a proper definition of 'moral', is what is ultimately beneficial to people. When damage is done, it is when emotions enter the picture. This is not to say that emotions are always bad, but that logic, properly used, can be said to be invariably good. If the NT do allow their emotions to be guided by logic, they must experience rewards that I cannot even begin to imagine.

It might be beneficial, at this point, to explicitly mention that doing this has not given me the 'warm and fuzzy' feelings that NT people seem to get out of many things that they do. (This sort of motivation, for me, might as well exist only in another galaxy. I know of its existence only through hearing the NT talk about it in such glowing terms.) My own motivation was that it was obviously the logical thing for me to do.

Temple Grandin has written[2] that she does not accept anything on faith. Neither do I. If there is a question the answer to which eludes me, I do not cease to search for an answer that would satisfy my sense of rationality. I realize that I might never find it during my earthly lifetime, but I do not stop looking. In fact, the closest verbal concept of God that I have ever heard was given by the medium in the motion picture *Poltergeist*: a great light in which is contained the answer to any question you might ever want to ask.

Concomitant with the rational structure of my religion is the belief that there is no all-encompassing master plan, but that, given both the laws of

2   Grandin, Temple: *op. cit.*, p.189

nature and humans' free will, what happens to us is pretty much the luck of the draw.

Yet, there are some thoughts, about what I have been doing for these parents, that do intrigue me. They concern those assaults that took place on my brain, at that early age when it was still in the process of being wired.

One is that, at that time, my autism could have been of the non-communicating variety. Since that happened about fifteen years before autism was first diagnosed, I would have been classed as hopelessly mentally retarded, and probably also have been institutionalized. Yet, I was spared that one particular affliction; my ability to communicate remained intact.

Another thought is that, when this happened, something was taken away from me, but I was also left with something else. The combination has allowed me to be able to express what goes on inside me and, thus, to be of help to parents whose children cannot do this.

In addition, when I was searching for activities to take up the slack in my life, one of the first things I did was to audition for a second high-powered choral group. I felt that this would double the pleasure I got from that type of activity. I had no problem qualifying, but they had no vacancies at the time.

That chorus rehearses on Tuesdays. Had I been able to join, my Tuesdays would have been completely booked. The first two support groups that I worked with met on Tuesdays. Since that day of the week would have been preempted, I could not have given any serious thought to working with the support groups.

In a large chorus, one voice, more or less, does not make any appreciable difference. From the reactions of those who are involved, I appear to have made a considerable contribution to the members of those groups.

Finally, I was also able to relate my schizophrenia misdiagnosis to those many sessions that I spent with that Benedictine priest when I underwent my conversion to Catholicism. (It must be remembered that, at that time, I had not the slightest inkling of being autistic.)

I was, at the time (as during most of my life), bewildered at my inability to fit in with any group. This seemed to also be true about the Church. The priest, not knowing of my autism, had wondered why I tended to intellectualize everything so much. Of course, I did not, at that time, realize that this was all I had to go on.

I told him how proud I was of those intellectual and aesthetic faculties. They had, after all, enabled me not only to make my way in what I saw as a hostile world, but also to enjoy it as others, in many ways, did not or could not. He told me that those things could be taken away from me at any time.

At that time, I scoffed at this. Yet, during those years of 'schizophrenia' (and the psychotropic drugs), while I did not lose those faculties, I was given a graphic illustration of what my life would be like had I lost them.

These things do keep, in the back of my mind, the thought that, for all of my rationality, God likes to remind me, every so often, that He sometimes does move in mysterious ways.

Isn't that a frightening thought?

Ezio Pinza as
the Czar Boris

DATE DUE

FEB 1 6 2000		
JAN 2 4 2000	OCT 2 0 2004	
APR 0 5 2000	NOV 1 7 2004	
APR 1 8 2000	DEC 1 7 2004	
APR 1 8 2000	JUN 11 2008	
	OCT 3 0 2012	
	DEC 1 8 2012	
MAR 0 7 2001	OCT 3 1 2013	
MAR 0 5 2001	DEC 1 6 2013	
APR 1 1 2001		
MAY 1 0 2001		
APR 2 0 2001		
MAY 0 8 2002		
APR 0 9 2002		
MAR 3 0 2005		
AUG 1 3 2008		
GAYLORD		PRINTED IN U.S.A.